CULTIVATING CHAOS

JONAS REIF | CHRISTIAN KRESS |
WITH PHOTOS BY JÜRGEN BECKER

CULTIVATING CHAOS

HOW TO ENRICH LANDSCAPES WITH SELF-SEEDING PLANTS

FOREWORD BY NOEL KINGSBURY

TIMBER PRESS
PORTLAND, OREGON

CONTENTS

Foreword   7

HOW DO YOU GARDEN WITH SELF-SEEDING PLANTS?   9

Letting go   11

The advantages of gardening with self-seeders   12
  Does this form of gardening require a lot of work? 15

The strategy behind self-seeding plants   16

The life spans of self-seeding plants   23
  Annuals   23
  Biennials   25
  Monocarpic plants   25
  Short-lived perennials   26
  Long-lived perennials   27

DUNGENESS – NATURE'S TAPESTRY   29

LET THE PLANTING BEGIN   45

Using seeds and plug plants   47
  Judging the quantity   47

Preparation for planting   48
  Improving the soil   48
  Planting out   49
  Sowing seed   50

Wolfram Kunick – the pioneer of pioneers   53

Transforming a site   54
  Reducing soil fertility   54
  Changing the surface structure   56
  Raising soil pH   57
  Lowering soil pH   59
  Further possibilities for transforming your soil   59

Gardening from the bottom up   60

HET VLACKELAND – FAST-BLOOMING DYNAMIC SPLENDOUR   63

STRATEGIES FOR DESIGN AND MAINTENANCE

79

Can self-seeding plants be controlled?   81

Unwanted plants   81

Every picture needs a frame   84
   The Dutch Wave gardeners   86

Ton ter Linden – chaotic charm in the garden   89

Plants in crevices and joints   91
   Horizontal surfaces   91
   Vertical surfaces   92

Crushed limestone beds   94

Meadows – cultivating chaos on a grand scale   96

Managing the mix   99
   Free bloomers   99
   Magnificence   99
   Gap-finders   100
   Salt of the earth   100

Picking your time   102
   The seedling phase   102

The growth phase   102
The start of flowering   105
During flowering   105
The end of flowering   106
After dropping seed   107

The only constant is change   108

WALTHAM PLACE – NATURALISM IN A FORMAL SETTING   111

PLANTS FOR SELF-SEEDING GARDENS

127

   Species for masonry joints, shingle and gravel beds   128
   Species for flower borders   140
   Species for sunny perennial plantings   152
   Species for partial and full shade   162

RESOURCES

177
   Nurseries   178
   Gardens to visit   178
   Further reading   179
   Index   180
   Afterword & acknowledgements   186
   The authors   187

Foreword

Once upon a time I bought a plant of *Geranium sylvaticum* 'Birch Lilac'. Nine years later, when I moved on from that particular garden, there must have been a hundred of them. It had seeded pretty well all over, so every year May became a haze of violet-blue. It was the perfect seeder, never over-doing it, and crucially, it being a relatively narrow plant, it never swamped anything else. Like many of the best self-seeding effects in gardens its behaviour was not predicted. And like many, when I tried to reproduce it in my next garden, the plant would only self-sow reluctantly.

Allowing and encouraging plants to set seed in the garden and spread themselves around is very much a part of the new garden zeitgeist. Once we planted things and expected them to stay where they were put. Gardening now is much more accepting of spontaneity, of natural processes of birth, death and decay. Embracing plants that self-seed is part of becoming a manager of nature rather than a controller. Seeding is a vital way in which plant communities thrive and survive. Allowing it in the garden can be seen as a way of the garden becoming an ecological system.

Self-seeding can be a mixed blessing of course. First there is the unpredictability. Although some, like *Aquilegia vulgaris*, seem to seed in most gardens, most species are not so obliging; they may seed well, or poorly, or not at all, or too much. The latter can be a problem, and there are certainly plants which I now regard as near weeds which started out as desired plants. The winter annual *Euphorbia rigida* is one. I was thrilled when I first saw seedlings, as I always am when a new plant does this – a sign that the species is at home, and that I have a real dynamic ecological system on my hands. But when the numbers increased, to start to clutter every piece of empty ground within seed-throwing distance of the parent, then I began to regret it, especially as the plants fell over as soon as they flower. Now, almost on the point of eliminating it, I step back from the brink, and let a few survive. In the denser vegetation of what is now a more established garden, they do not seed so much, they have to compete for resources and are more likely to be supported by neighbours. But I will continue to watch them.

Managing the mysteries of self-seeders engages the gardener in the ongoing process of the garden's own independent life, and is a reminder of the wider world of natural systems, of which the garden can be a tiny and homely example. It is good to have a book that recognises the importance of this vital ecological process. Self-seeding can be a little alarming to the nervous or the novice, and advice from experienced managers of the process is most valuable.

Noel Kingsbury

Alcea rosea (hollyhock), *Cichorium intybus* (chicory) and *Verbascum* spp. (mullein) surround a traditional house on the island of Bornholm in the Baltic Sea. Just a few centimetres of soil and shelter from a projecting eave are enough to provide the right conditions for a lively border full of flowers.

How do you garden with self-seeding plants?

Managing a garden that relies on self-seeding plants for effect differs greatly from the traditional approach to gardening. It considers planning and maintenance as interlinked and works with nature rather than against it. Dynamic change and chance play important roles in this process, as do the choice of plants and the willingness to work with forces that are outside our control.

Letting go

Traditional gardening is a means by which we attempt to control plants and get them to do what we want. So what happens when we let go of this natural instinct to control our environment?

Scientists of behavioural biology call a system that can only be observed from outside a "black box". The black box is a metaphor for those physical and cognitive processes that cannot (yet) be scientifically described. The magnitude and scope of a black box's influence as well as its output can be measured, but the exact manner in which that black box functions remains unclear.

A garden left to natural processes behaves in much the same way as a black box. Although you may understand how on-site conditions such as soil, light and moisture will affect growth and you can locate and identify "seed providers", it is impossible to predict which seedling will appear where and in what quantities – the variables are too numerous and diverse.

In fact, when we leave a garden to its natural devices it is the unexpected that amazes us again and again. A plant that we haven't seen in years suddenly appears; another plant blooms heroically one year and then disappears the next; plants interbreed to produce new colours and shapes that we haven't seen before.

In conventional garden planning, the details of planting for each area are drawn up and the species are positioned and planted accordingly. The gardener's role is then to care for the group plantings so that they look as they should and to maintain the garden in this state for as long as possible. But when gardening with self-seeders, you may begin with just a notion of how the garden might look. Instead of placing numerous plants at precise, final locations according to a plan, you introduce plants to the garden in the form of seeds or plug plants. In time, their progeny seek out spots in the garden where they can thrive long-term. In this way, a planting establishes itself naturally and the gardener's role is simply to guide the process by the removal of individual plants or patches where they become too dominant. In order to establish a wide range of plants, which is often the goal of the gardener, it is possible to adapt sites in the garden according to the needs of particular species.

The more species-rich your garden is, and the more particular your creative goals, the more your garden will require appropriate, well-timed intervention, and continual observation. Gardening with self-seeding plants uses standard gardening knowledge and techniques in a slightly different way to produce gardens that are constantly changing and very much alive. Are you ready to experiment?

Flower meadows occur only when competitive plants are unable to survive because of climate or human interference. Crested Butte is a favourite winter sport destination in Colorado, USA. Among the many plants to be found in summer on its diverse mountain meadows are *Aquilegia caerulea* (columbine), *Lupinus argenteus* (lupin) and *Castilleja linariifolia* (Indian paintbrush).

The advantages of gardening with self-seeders

Traditional gardening has worked successfully for centuries, so why would you want to change the way you have always gardened?

This is a legitimate question, but times have changed and so have our ideas and desired outcomes for gardens. Here are some of the advantages of gardening with self-seeders:

— Quick results. The extra time needed for germination and extensive production of seed is quickly repaid. Many plants flower in the first or second year and then become permanent residents in the garden.
— A colourful and flower-rich garden. Many self-seeders are short-lived and are therefore oriented towards multiplying abundantly. In nature, this is most successfully done by the production of profuse, vividly coloured flowers and numerous seeds.
— You will tune into nature. When gardening with self-seeders, you become an intimate observer of a plant's life cycle, watching it germinate, grow, bloom, set fruit, set seed and wilt. In this way you discover the true character of plants that have not been touched by constant pruning and other intervention. Also, self-seeding plants are rich in food sources and habitats for wildlife.
— You can enjoy a cultivated chaos. By adding new species and removing superfluous plants, you can design your garden to match your aesthetics. This does not mean dogmatically restricting yourself to native plant species – though all environmentally conscious gardeners need to be aware of the dangers of introducing opportunistic plants outside their native environments.
— Versatility. Self-seeding plants can be used in a traditional garden design as well as in this newer informal style.
— It can be done just about anywhere. Gardening with self-seeders works in mature and virgin gardens alike. In fact, you don't even need a garden, for seeds will germinate wherever humus can collect, whether on balconies, in the cracks of paved walkways, in the joints of a brick or stone wall or on a flat, gravel-covered roof.
— It offers an element of surprise. As there is no garden plan to realize and no precious plants to lose, there's practically no way to fail. On the contrary, unexpected results are intriguing and stimulating.
— It is inexpensive. Instead of purchasing a large number of established plants, all you need are a few plug plants or seeds.
— It is suitable for beginners too. There is little to learn beforehand and what you do need to know you will find in this book. Many of the species are relatively easy to establish in the garden.

Short-lived plants are biologically programmed to produce seed prolifically. Insects benefit from this as well in the form of increased availability of nectar and seeds.

Self-seeders can be cultivated even in small spaces; here, *Viola odorata* (violet) grows on a balcony.

Locally acquired seeds, either collected or bought, are holiday souvenirs that keep on giving.

Self-seeding plants are an important feature at Great Dixter, East Sussex, England. Maintaining such a garden year in and year out requires highly qualified gardeners who have an understanding of the ethos behind its cultivation.

Does this form of gardening require a lot of work?

As with many gardening questions, the answer is "It all depends ..." The most important maintenance tasks consist of observing growth and, if necessary, reducing the numbers of certain plants. Physically demanding work is only necessary in those cases when you wish to drastically change the site. Special tools are not required; everything you need to do can be carried out with a pair of garden shears and a spade. So, maintenance is pretty easy.

However, gardening with self-seeding plants means ensuring that their seeds can land on appropriate surfaces – patches of open soil or gravel. Open, aerated soils are also quickly populated by unwanted species such as those generally considered to be weeds, though many don't do so well on surfaces covered with gravel or grit. These will need to be removed, and that, of course, means work.

Start small

— Perhaps you already have self-seeding plants in your garden? Just looking at them more closely and making a few specific changes will bring rapid results.
— Try getting seeds to germinate in the cracks between paving slabs or joints in stone or brickwork. Alternatively, start a gravel bed. Populating open soil with lush self-seeding plants is something for the more experienced gardener.
— You can produce a very impressive-looking garden with just a few species. You can always add more later!
— Use plants that are easily recognizable by their leaves or growth habit. This will help you to distinguish them from weeds.

A *Peucedanum verticillare* (giant hog fennel or milk parsley)
B *Geranium pratense* (meadow cranesbill)
C *Geranium pratense* subsp. *alba* (white-flowered meadow cranesbill)
D *Aquilegia vulgaris* 'Alba' (white columbine)
E *Pastinaca sativa* (parsnip)
F *Hesperis matronalis* (dame's violet)
G *Verbascum* 'Christo's Yellow Lightning' (verbascum)
H *Allium christophii* (star of Persia)
J *Allium aflatunense* (ornamental onion)
K *Gladiolus communis* subsp. *byzantinus* (Byzantine gladiolus or Jacob's ladder)
L *Foeniculum vulgare* 'Atropurpureum' (bronze fennel)
M *Geranium pratense* (meadow cranesbill)
N *Dipsacus fullonum* (Fuller's teasel or wild teasel)
O *Geranium pratense* subsp. *alba* (white meadow cranesbill)

The strategy behind self-seeding plants

All living things in nature are designed to perpetuate their species. Plants have two ways of going about this: generatively, that is, via seeds, and vegetatively, for example by means of runners or by forming new bulbs. The combination of both generative and vegetative reproduction is also possible. The reproductive method of a plant depends largely on its survival strategy, site conditions and competitive situation.

To better describe the behaviour of plants, scientists developed various models. One well-respected model came from the British ecologist John Philip Grime. He differentiated between competitive plants, which have an advantage on sites with ideal conditions; stress-tolerant species, which are able to grow despite deficiencies in light, moisture or nutrients; and ruderal plants, which are adapted to thrive in disturbed areas and can survive partial or complete loss of their vegetation.

On closer inspection of this last group, two completely different paths emerge: on the one hand there are plants that survive disturbance as a group being one organism, such as a lawn that becomes denser with regular mowing, or plants in a pasture that livestock selectively graze. Plants such as *Gymnocarpium robertianum* (limestone oak fern) also survive in this way by sending up rhizomes after being covered in landslides.

On the other hand there are plants that survive disturbance not as an organism but as a species. They survive life-extinguishing events, which may be small or large scale and may last for years, through seed production. Especially good conditions often follow such events, with plenty of light, sufficient nutrients and little competition. Speed of growth is the key to take advantage of these conditions.

Another group of plants uses beneficial situations in much the same way, avoiding stress and competition by forming biotic communities and occupying a specific niche. Here it is also important to be in the right place at the right time, and nothing fits the bill better than the production of seed, as illustrated below and right.

At some sites, even experts are puzzled as to how plants arrived, to say nothing of how they survive. Here, *Pseudofumaria lutea* (yellow corydalis) seems to be finding everything it needs.

Barren deserts in the southwestern United States can transform into colourful landscapes after an intense spring rainstorm. Since precipitation is not guaranteed every year, plants need an appropriate strategy to survive. This picture comes from the Organ Pipe Cactus National Monument in Arizona and shows *Eschscholzia californica* subsp. *mexicana* (California poppy) and *Lupinus sparsiflorus* (Coulter's lupin). Comparable species can also be cultivated on well-drained sites in Europe.

— Many sites are difficult for plants to reach. Only a very small number of species are able to scale a rock face by sending up runners. Seeds, which may be transported by others, represent the more practical strategy. Ants and birds are usually the most dependable modes of transport, depositing seed deep in a protected crevice or providing a little fertilizer in the form of droppings.

— Agricultural fields are disturbance sites *par excellence*. No plant survives the plough, but most seeds do. If a plant is to establish itself alongside field crops, it needs to germinate, grow, bloom and fruit within a few weeks.

— Deserts, with their aridity, heat, cold and soil salinity, are hostile to life, but many of these regions are transformed by a powerful rainstorm. Within a few days, thousands of plants sprout from the barren ground, their colourful flowers briefly lighting up the landscape before disappearing. Yet this short period is enough for the plants to go through their entire life cycle, concluding with the setting of seed, thus securing the next generation even if a few years pass before the next rainfall.

— Flooding along rivers and coastlines leads to repeated cycles of erosion and deposition of sand and gravel. Depending on the amount of water, nutrients and seeds in the soil, these seeds can quickly populate the area. Early colonizers are able to stay until they are suppressed by more competitive species or until high water again comes and washes everything away. Flooding may be less common today because of a greater degree of human intervention in the flow of rivers, but ever-increasing construction projects expose more and more soil to be populated by more early colonizers.

Fields of red poppies are the epitome of an idyllic countryside. Re-creating this in the garden requires disruption of the soil every year.

— In a broad-leaved forest, large tree canopies prevent much light from reaching the ground in summer, so other plants wishing to thrive need to start earlier in the year. Plants that have sent up shoots and bloomed by early spring are undisturbed by the unfurling of tree leaves a month later. Even where there seems to be no trace of light, unexpected gaps in the form of wind damage or logging could appear. Since such opportunities are completely unpredictable, seeds need to survive long periods in the ground and ideally are distributed throughout the forest.

— Meadows are usually dominated by competitive, long-lived grasses. Sometimes, however, when insufficient nutrients are present in the soil, or there is little rainfall, or the grasses are inhibited by parasitic plants, small amounts of soil become exposed at the surface. This is often enough for some seeds to germinate and establish a new plant.

Whereas Grime compared and contrasted the factors of competition, stress and rapid propagation, the graphic below focuses on four plant strategies. However, few plants at any stage in their life follow just one strategy. Instead, each finds its own method of survival. Plants that are ideal for the cultivating-chaos approach to gardening are primarily those found in the "Evaders" corner.

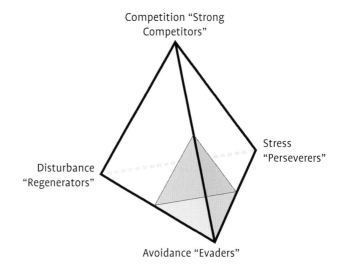

Competition "Strong Competitors"

Stress "Perseverers"

Disturbance "Regenerators"

Avoidance "Evaders"

Digitalis purpurea (purple foxglove) springs up en masse in forests only after felling or large-scale wind damage to trees. Since such events are rare, the seeds must survive for years in the soil.

Epilobium dodonaei (alpine willowherb) is native to southern Europe and grows in poor soils such as dry river beds. A flood could disturb its environment but would also remove the competition..

Plants regarded as weeds in conventional agriculture bring gardens to life, as here with *Centaurea cyanus* (cornflower) and *Papaver rhoeas* (field poppy). If you consider cultivating these, bear in mind the annual disturbance of the soil that will be needed and their relatively short flowering time.

It's easy to concentrate too much attention on the flowering stage of a plant's life cycle, which may not last long. Some species, such as *Tragopogon porrifolius* (purple salsify), produce inconspicuous flowers but enrich the garden with decorative buds and seed heads.

The life spans of self-seeding plants

Although all self-seeding plants follow similar strategies, they have different life spans which influence how they are used and maintained in the garden. Depending on the site, the difference in cultivating biennials, monocarpic plants (plants that flower once and then die) and short-lived perennials may be minimal. When biennials and perennials bloom in the following years, they often do so less profusely than in the first.

Annuals

These plants are unable to survive heat, drought and low light levels and instead remain dormant during these times in seed form. So-called winter annuals germinate in autumn and flower the following spring. The strategy-influencing period of disadvantage in the case of these is not the winter, but rather the warmer time in spring, when strong competitive pressures prevail.

Annuals are notable for their profuse flowering. Where they appear en masse in the wild, they can dominate the colour of large areas of landscape. Herein lies their potential: with their impressive flowers and, to some extent, interesting textures, they can be used to define a large area of the garden.

As a rule, annuals are introduced to the garden by sowing seed, though in exceptional cases it may be appropriate to plant seedlings. Encouraging them to establish and spread means waiting until the plants start to drop new seed. It will be necessary to clear the soil in the area populated by these plants once a year to maintain them, though merely clearing an area for establishing new plants may not suffice for all species, some of which may require some tilling or loosening of the soil.

— Examples: *Eschscholzia californica* (California poppy), *Papaver rhoeas* (corn poppy) and *Myosotis sylvatica* (forget-me-not).

Biennials

Plants in this group usually live for two vegetation periods: in the first year they germinate and establish themselves, then in the following year they flower, set seed and die.

Like annuals, biennials survive unfavourable periods in seed form, though they are not found at such extreme sites. In general, biennials are more robust than annuals. Morphological adaptations such as tap roots and hairy leaves and stems enable them to survive the winter and periods of drought.

Biennials are desirable for their impressive growth habits and interesting structures. Their flowers can be very attractive, but they are mostly not as extravagant as those of annuals. Many species are superb all-rounders that establish quickly to great effect and add character to the whole garden.

Establish biennials in the garden by sowing seed or using plug plants that are available in summer. It is better to use recently germinated plants because plants in the second year of vegetation do not do nearly as well. Wait for the plants to drop seed before cutting them back once the flowers are over.

Maintaining the plants requires an annual turning of the soil to dislodge competing plants and it is also important to keep a portion of the soil surface bare so that new plants can become established.

— Examples: *Verbascum olympicum* (mullein) and *Digitalis purpurea* (foxglove).

Monocarpic plants

Plants of this group are very similar to biennial plants in that they both build up stores of energy that they then use up for seed production, followed shortly by the death of the plant. What sets these plants apart from biennials is that the process can be drawn out over several years. Monocarpic plants are also known as hapaxanths or semelparous organisms.

Like biennials, monocarpic plants are known for their impressive growth habits and inflorescence and interesting plant structures: they are appropriate for defining distinct garden spaces, which they can do quickly.

Introduce monocarpic plants into the garden as seed or young plants and wait for the plant to drop seed before cutting it back. Maintain them in the garden by regular disturbance of the soil or by keeping clear the surface of the bed where you establish them.

— Examples: *Angelica gigas* (purple angelica) and *A. archangelica* (angelica), *Peucedanum verticillare* (giant hog fennel or milk parsley).

If you provide *Angelica archangelica* (angelica) with bare soil to drop its seeds on, you will have it in the garden for decades. It needs different amounts of space as it goes from sprouting to flowering, which you will need to provide for, as here in combination with *Digitalis purpurea* (foxglove).

Short-lived perennials

Short-lived perennials survive one or more flowering cycles. Limited nutrient availability and the absence of competition lengthens their lives. They are typically the "second wave" of succession (see box). They can live a few years before being forced out by more competitive plants. With similar virtues to the monocarpic plants, they can be used to give character to individual garden spaces.

Plant some plug plants or sow seed to introduce them into the garden and wait for part of the plant to drop seed before cutting them back. Regular disturbance or keeping an establishment patch cleared are required for maintenance.

— Examples: *Oenothera odorata* (evening primrose), *Lychnis coronaria* (rose campion).

Natural Succession

Natural succession refers to the process of change in the vegetation of a site over time. In general, this happens when a site is newly populated by plants after a major disturbance, such as a flood or deposition of a new soil layer. Succession does not come to an end until the emergence of a so-called climax community (such as beech forest in central Europe). Leading up to the climax community are several stages: annual and biennial pioneer plants are followed by perennial forbs and shrubs until the site becomes a forest. Plants of early successional stages are known as ruderal flora.

If you have enough space, you can experiment with allowing larger shrubs to spread seed, as here with *Miscanthus sinensis* (Chinese silver grass), perennial *Helianthus* spp. (sunflower) and *Deschampsia cespitosa* (tufted hairgrass). Be aware that robust, long-lived perennials can potentially get out of hand and spread further than you wish. If this is a concern for you, limit each grass or tall-growing *Helianthus* species to one each in the garden, which will keep the amount of seed to a minimum.

Long-lived perennials

These plants can live to be very old and are characteristic of mature gardens (see box). In the medium and long term, they give the garden an unmistakable character. At the same time, these are the most challenging plants to cultivate in the self-sown garden, since much patience is required before they fully populate their designated sites.

Nevertheless, long-lived perennials are easiest to introduce to the garden as plants. It is possible to use seed, though their seeds often germinate inconsistently or slowly. While perennials need not reproduce themselves in the same quantities as annuals or biennials, a certain amount of regular seed production is nonetheless required for maintaining the species. Perennial seedlings take much more time – more than three years is not unusual – until the first flowering and need to be selectively freed from competition. Most species grow in clumps, though a few spread by sending out runners. Fully grown plants no longer need your support, so you should avoid disturbing them at this stage.

— Examples: *Alchemilla mollis* (lady's mantle), *Helleborus* × *hybridus* (Christmas rose).

A mature garden

Gardens with fully grown trees and borders of long-lived perennials are generally known as mature gardens. The presence of numerous plants that have filled appropriate ecological niches is another characteristic attribute.

Helleborus orientalis hybrids produce moderate amounts of seed. Depending on local conditions, it can take four to ten years for a germinated seed to grow into a flowering plant. As for many other plants, it is not necessary to prepare the soil. You can count on the seed producing plants except where highly competitive ground-cover plants are present.

DUNGENESS – NATURE'S TAPESTRY

opposite:
At Dungeness, the exposed strips of shingle show how the peninsula was formed by successive storm surges. As the peninsula grew by several metres a year, the lighthouse needed to be periodically replaced.

left:
Crambe maritima (sea kale) presents a fascinating display of colours throughout the year.

Dungeness is a small peninsula in Kent, England that juts into the English Channel. The subsoil consists of pebbles, between which little or no humus is able to collect. The climate in this location is decidedly mild. Due to the low annual precipitation – 625 mm (24½ in) per year – and the poor water retention of the shingle, trees and shrubs are unable to establish here, making Dungeness England's only desert. Several plants are, however, able to take up moisture from the fog and the salty sea spray and store it in their foliage. These conditions have led to the establishment of a unique flora.

Some 600 species – about a quarter of the total number of species present in England – are found in this area of less than 20 km² (7¾ square miles). Many of the plants have a short lifespan, the difficult conditions forcing them into a strategy of seed production for survival. However, because of the mild winters, plants can be seen at Dungeness that one would not expect to find in most places in the UK.

The southern part of the peninsula is accessible to visitors via a private road through the Dungeness Estate. There are many plants to discover, whether out towards the sea or further inland. If you would like to explore Dungeness, plan for at least one full day to experience both a sunrise and a sunset.

At first glance, Dungeness seems to be a desolate wasteland of rusting metal huts, old fishing boats which have not touched seawater in years, machines for long-forgotten uses and vast expanses of land and sky. Yet if you look closer, a stunning diversity of plants is revealed.

The Road to Nowhere leads through a field of *Crambe maritima* (sea kale). Its roots reach several metres into the soil to ensure its survival, even when there is no rain for several weeks. Although the ground may appear flat, a walk across the shingle requires much time and energy.

Dungeness displays an intense array of colours in the summer months. A brilliant blue is provided here by *Echium vulgare* (viper's bugloss). It remains a mystery as to whether the salt contents of the soil or the strong coastal light incidence are responsible for its intense hue, or whether it is just the contrast with the subdued tones of the surroundings.

Dungeness is a place of great diversity. Among the plants found here are some unexpected ones, such as *Iris orientalis* (Spuria iris), which is native to an area from central and southern Europe to Iran and Algeria.

Glaucium flavum (yellow hornpoppy) tends to grow in dense, narrow stands, often just above the tideline in coastal areas.

Reseda luteola (weld or dyer's rocket) is a native of western Asia and the Mediterranean but it was cultivated in many countries as the source of bright yellow dye.

Digitalis purpurea (purple foxglove) is a plant you would not normally expect to find in a shingle habitat, but here it appears to be doing very well.

opposite:
A warm, radiant pink is not often seen in the flora of Dungeness, but the flowers of *Papaver somniferum* (opium poppy), originally from the eastern Mediterranean, fit in with the landscape.

top left:
Antirrhinum majus (snapdragons) come in many different colours, appearing year after year.

middle left:
Lathyrus latifolius (everlasting pea) comes from southern Europe and was first noted in Dungeness in 1988. Since then it has spread along the entire coastline.

bottom left:
Kniphofia species (red-hot pokers) do so well in the local climate that they sometimes escape out of the gardens here. Conservationists have instituted control measures to prevent them from becoming too invasive.

top right:
At Dungeness, *Linaria purpurea* (purple toadflax) blooms in an incomparably intense hue.

middle right:
Sedum album (white stonecrop) demonstrates that stress can have benefits; its leaves turn red in response to lack of rainfall and saline soils.

bottom right:
Sedum acre (biting stonecrop) is found throughout Europe, particularly in sandy or stony soils.

opposite:
Against the backdrop of a nuclear power plant – whose impact on the exceptional plant life causes much speculation – a colourful potpourri of *Centranthus ruber* in diverse shades, *Echium vulgare* and *Papaver rhoeas* has established itself. In the background, the yellow flowers of *Ulex europaeus* (gorse) can be seen.

In 1986, British artist and film director Derek Jarman moved to Dungeness after being diagnosed with HIV. He fell in love with a black fisherman's cottage with brilliant yellow window frames that happened to be for sale at the time and Dungeness increasingly became the focal point of his life. An enthusiastic gardener since childhood, Jarman allowed his shingle garden to develop naturally. He established "beds" by laying lighter-coloured gravel in rectangles and circles and concentrating on self-seeding plants such as *Eschscholzia californica* (California poppy). In the foreground, *Centranthus ruber* (red valerian) blooms.

A "formal garden" made from twelve railway sleepers was created to the side of the cottage. *Crambe maritima* (sea kale) and a few *Centranthus ruber* (red valerian) plants are all that grow between the sleepers. Just visible in the distance is the omnipresent nuclear power plant.

The garden is a mixture of naturally occurring plants, introduced species and odds and ends washed up from the beach, all artfully arranged by Derek Jarman. In the rear garden there is a small area that is shielded from the constant wind by the cottage. As a result of planning combined with happy accident, *Santolina chamaecyparissus* (cotton lavender), *Crambe maritima* (sea kale), *Kniphofia* species (red-hot poker), *Centranthus ruber* (red valerian), *Digitalis purpurea* (foxglove) and in the rear a bright yellow brassica all bloom together.

While in the "formal" front garden most plants bear orange flowers, yellow dominates the garden at the back, as in this beautiful combination of *Eschscholzia californica* (California poppy) and *Glaucium flavum* (yellow hornpoppy).

Dungeness is the largest shingle habitat in the world and it might seem far-fetched to use its rich diversity as a model for the domestic garden. Yet a bit of Dungeness can be found anywhere – there is always a desolate patch that with a few amendments can be made far more wonderful than when it first meets the eye.

LET THE PLANTING BEGIN

Self-sown gardens are alive and full of flowers. Even though they seem profoundly natural, very few plants arrive in the garden without human intervention. What can you do, then, to introduce the plants you want into the garden? And, perhaps more importantly, how can you make their new home so desirable that they stay for the long haul?

Using seeds and plug plants

When you are establishing a garden with self-seeding plants there is a lot to be said for starting with seed, since compared with "pre-grown" plants it is inexpensive and easy to order by mail. As a general rule, use seed when the species germinates easily and needs no special treatment. This is the case for nearly all annual, biennial and monocarpic plants. Many short-lived perennials are also unproblematic. For long-lived perennials, check the details of the germination process before purchasing. Seed companies will be able to help you with the pertinent information.

In some cases, there is a good reason for using plug plants instead of seed. These will be the "mother" plants that spread their "children" throughout the garden. There are, of course, also species that are introduced in the garden via bulbs and tubers.

Depending upon the species and the particular strategy it uses, some seed can quickly lose its viability (that is, ability to germinate). By contrast, plug plants develop quickly and flower before plants grown from seed in the same year. They are also an ideal choice when you do not have a suitable place in the garden for seeds to germinate. For recommendations on which style of plant establishment is most likely to succeed, see the individual plant descriptions beginning on p.127.

Sometimes, the most simple reasons make plug plants the better option: you have, for example, just purchased this book in July and you want to start your self-seeding garden immediately rather than waiting until next spring!

Judging the quantity

When you are sowing seed, first work out the quantity you need to sow to achieve the spread of plants you want. If you are buying seed from a specialist seed company, the smallest amount they offer is usually the best choice; in a garden centre, simply buy a packet. Unless you are planning to turn your entire garden into a sea of flowers within one year, buying more seed just doesn't make sense. When conditions are right, your plants will spread quickly and create the desired effect on their own.

Recommendations about the appropriate number of plug plants are more difficult to make. Essentially, the longer-lived the species and the faster you want them to take over the garden, the more plants you will need. Yet, planting out on a scale that fills the entire garden is against the whole principle of gardening with self-seeding plants.

For plants with underground storage organs such as bulbs and tubers (known as geophytes), you should start with roughly the quantity you want to see in the garden. Packages of 100 or 1000 bulbs often cost no more than a mid-sized shrub from the garden centre, while most bulbs and tubers grown from seed take three to six years to produce flowers, so the choice here is obvious.

Hieracium villosum (shaggy hawkweed), with its characteristic woolly-haired leaves, thrives especially well in crushed limestone. From a single plant, it can form a ground-covering carpet within three years thanks to its prolific seed production.

Preparation for planting

Nothing is more effective for producing good results in the long term than thorough preparation of the soil before planting. Most perennials only grow well in cleared, tilled soil. The same is also true for plug plants that are intended to spread by self-seeding.

Good soil preparation can be done in every season and in every kind of soil. The most sensible approach to this is to break up the soil of the bed to about the depth of the spade. Digging heavy clay soils in autumn is effective as the freshly turned surface can freeze in the winter. This makes it easier for you to incorporate compost in spring, which in turn makes the soil more friable and overall a friendlier environment for perennials.

Digging out tap-rooted weeds is especially important, as they use reserves stored in their roots and sprout readily, even when their tops have been removed or when the top 50 cm (20 in) layer of soil has been replaced. Unfortunately, it is precisely this type of weed that is also the most resistant to herbicides. Although it's a long process (taking at least a full growing season before the soil is ready to sow or plant) sheet mulching with a material that provides complete shade and does not allow water to penetrate is extremely effective at killing weeds of all kinds.

Improving the soil

Compost is an excellent solution for long-term care of the soil, though commercially available hoof and horn meal, or bone meal, are also effective. It is difficult to give short-lived ruderal species too much compost, as they hunger for anything that speeds their development. Apply compost more sparingly to slower-growing species, as too much compost can lead them to over extend themselves and also encourage unwanted, highly competitive plants.

For plants that are adapted to lighter, poorer soils, you should refrain from adding compost at all and you will need to add sand or grit to the soil to further "dilute" it. Alternatively, you can start from scratch to establish a new gravel or grit bed.

In partial shade such as woodland edge, your approach to soil improvement should take into account the individual location. The primary concern is whether flat-rooted or tap-rooted woody plants are present. It is possible to dig the soil around tap-rooted trees, but where plug plants are to be set out beneath flat-rooted trees such as birch or maple, digging is all but impossible. Instead, bring in a new humus layer, about 15–20 cm (6–8 in) deep, and plant out into this, with closer than normal spacing if you wish. Follow the same method for sowing seed around smaller flat-rooted woody plants as well, although the humus layer can be somewhat thinner.

Planting out

Planting out is done in the traditional way. The only difference is that the number of plants per square metre can be kept to an absolute minimum.

Where there are nutrient-poor or coarse substrates such as gravel or grit, wash the soil from the rootball before planting. This minimizes the "flowerpot effect" where plants do not send out any new roots into the surrounding soil and are thus much more vulnerable to drought, prolonged rain and cold.

In conventional garden beds, a layer of mulch is applied after planting. Depending on what was planted, the mulch may consist of conifer bark, gravel, brick chippings or other material. The presence of sediment in gravel or other mineral groundcovers helps with germination, whereas bark mulch inhibits germination making it an excellent choice to control weeds in conventional gardens. For the self-sown garden, however, bark mulch is more of a hindrance than a help and should not be used.

Take great care in the preparation of planting surfaces. The ideal is to break up the soil in autumn and allow the topsoil to freeze over winter before using a rake to establish a fine tilth the following spring.

Sowing seed

Using seed rather than plug plants allows you to watch your developing plants from germination right through to full growth. Seed is sown either directly in the garden or in seed trays.

Most herbaceous perennials can be sown directly in open soil. The best time for sowing is autumn or early spring, when the soil stays moist longer and cool temperatures encourage the germination process. Umbellifers (Apiaceae) and tap-rooted perennials in particular should be sown directly in the area where you want them to remain as they are very difficult to transplant later. Simply dig the soil and then use a rake to give the surface a fine crumb structure. Working in some coarse sand improves success with germination. Sowing seed too densely leads to more work later, as you will need to thin out the seedlings, so don't be overgenerous with distribution. Except in the case of smaller seeds, such as *Digitalis* (foxglove), cover the seed lightly with soil. Water carefully and if the weather is dry water again lightly so that the germination process can proceed uninterrupted.

Seeds that germinate at low temperatures are best sown in autumn and winter, but the later the sowing, the lower the germination rate. Germination will be most successful when sown directly after the seeds ripen on the plants. An alternative is to simulate cold outdoor temperatures by putting seeds in the refrigerator for up to six weeks, depending on the species. However, simply storing a seed packet in the refrigerator is not enough to induce germination. The seeds must be first moistened and, ideally, sown in a seed tray.

Sowing in containers does have the advantage of increasing germination rates, but requires the extra step of potting on, unless seedlings are planted out directly in the garden.

Observation of container-grown seeds

To establish plants in the garden by seed, sow small amounts in a seed tray or a window box and label them. There are two advantages to this: you can test the viability of the seed and, perhaps more importantly, you gain a close view of the plants that will be in your garden. What do the cotyledons look like? And the first true leaves? Differentiating between wanted and unwanted plants can be difficult even for experienced gardeners; knowing exactly what your plants look like will help you to avoid mistaking them for weeds and pulling them out.

Also, a window box can also serve as a sort of Noah's ark, making it easy to save plants if late frosts strike the seeds that are germinating in the garden.

Whether grown in a seed tray or a flower pot, you will gain information about the quality of the seed and how the plants will look in the garden by observing sprouting seeds and seedlings.

Wolfram Kunick – the pioneer of pioneers

Dr Wolfram Kunick was one of the first people to recognize the creative potential of self-seeding plants and to use them in the garden. Born in Leipzig, he witnessed how the mounds of debris left by World War II were greened by plant growth without human intervention. These were completely different plants to the ones he knew from his parents' garden and his horticultural training on the island of Mainau in Lake Constance. In Berlin, which was still littered with war damage and where he later studied garden design, he again came in contact with pioneer plant species. This fascinated him to such a degree that he mapped Berlin's areas of natural growth for his doctorate. He later mapped urban biotopes in other German cities, including Bremerhaven, Cologne, Stuttgart and Karlsruhe.

In 1985 Kunick became Professor of Open Space Planning and Urban Ecology at the University of Kassel. He left after seven years of teaching to grow annuals and perennials in a field near Bonn. A catalyst for this move was a visit in 1992 from the Dutch garden philosopher and seed producer Rob Leopold, who introduced Kunick to a wealth of exotic plants from all corners of the earth.

Kunick continued with his design and consultation work and for the National Garden Show in Magdeburg in 1999 he designed a meadow of wild perennials that received much admiration from the public and professionals alike. To research this project, a large field was seeded and planted. By regularly taking a census of the field, Kunick attempted to understand how the planting changed over time. The insights he gained from this serve to optimize maintenance of the meadow and also influence the planning of new projects, such as sowing perennial seeds for the State Garden Show in Zülpich, Germany, in 2014.

Wolfram Kunick's garden in Bornheim serves as a field for experimentation and also a place to produce seed for various projects. For the Vorgebirgspark in Cologne, he combined typical self-seeding perennials such as *Oenothera glazioviana* (red-sepal evening primrose) and *Verbascum* species (mullein) with annual ornamentals such as *Rudbeckia hirta* (black-eyed susan).

Transforming a site

All gardens have sunny and shady areas; some parts may lie a bit lower than others and the soil here may be somewhat cooler; under the eaves, dry conditions may prevail. A certain degree of plant diversity will be possible if you clear one site, but you can do much more to increase diversity if you establish a range of different sites in the garden.

The soil itself presents the greatest opportunity for change. In traditional gardening, much can be done here – though usually only in one direction: by adding fertilizer, the amount of nutrients and thereby the rate of plant growth can be increased. The presence of nutrients plays an important role for self-seeding plants too, but just as important are low-nutrient, open sites that are free of competition and ready for germination. In nature, these patches are found in ecological niches that can be re-created in the garden to a certain degree. You won't need an entire beach or the Alps to get started!

Reducing soil fertility

Conservationists have long known that sites with nutrient-poor soils are rich with diversity. Here, highly competitive species starve and are unable to form a dense blanket of vegetation – in meadows these are mostly grasses. In the spaces between plants, various species that are accustomed to poor soils are able to establish. To achieve a similar effect in the garden, you will need plenty of space – and before you begin, ask yourself if impoverishing the soil will truly achieve the desired effect. If,

If you eat a lot of mussels, use the leftover shells to make a "maritime" bed. If you don't have enough shells, combine them with lime grit to bulk them up.

for example, you have humus-poor sandy soils to begin with, diluting the nutrients in the soil further will probably not bring any major changes to the garden.

Most people do not want to spend years removing organic matter from the soil, and a sensible alternative is to exchange the top 10 cm (4 in) of soil for fine-grained sand or grit. Alternatively, you can add the 10 cm (4 in) layer of sand or grit on top or mix it into the existing topsoil. Carefully pouring sand or grit onto the soil surface between plants is also possible, though less effective. As nutrients are likely to accumulate again over time, the soil will need to be amended on a regular basis.

Removing the topsoil was done for centuries in agricultural landcapes with the intention of collecting nutrient- and

humus-rich soils and using them elsewhere to increase crop yields. Here, the purpose is to expose the underlying nutrient-poor subsoil. Because of the lack of competition, a plethora of pioneer species are then able to establish.

In Louis le Roy's Ecokathedraal at Mildam in the Netherlands, there is a brick rubble bed for self-seeding plants. Although *Geranium robertianum* (herb robert) can be seen here it is not recommended for self-seeding gardens because of its odour and tendency to spread aggressively.

Changing the surface structure

To keep flowers coming in the long term, you will need to create garden spaces that remain clear of vegetation. The basic rule is that wherever something is to germinate, there must be light and water. Digging is an option, or for larger spaces, you could rotovate, harrow or plough. This may sound crude, and indeed it is, but in this way you can maintain a few beautiful, familiar species such as *Papaver rhoeas* (poppy) and *Aquilegia* (columbine) – although remember that many weeds are also pioneer species that can readily populate newly disturbed soils.

Gravel gardens have become popular in recent years. Along the edges, where gravel or grit is only a few centimetres deep, or where a little humus has accumulated between the rocks, the seeds of self-seeding plants germinate particularly well. To some extent, such sites are comparable with railway tracks or gravel-covered flat roofs. Many plants of Mediterranean origin are well adapted to the conditions found in gravel gardens and populate them almost effortlessly: the gravel warms quickly and passes this stored heat on to plants. Additionally, it serves as a capillary break, preventing moisture from rising out of the soil. Since water is not being drawn up to the soil surface where it can evaporate, it is available for use by plants.

There is no hard and fast rule about how deep the layer of gravel should be. A layer of variable depth lends itself to higher diversity than one of consistent depth. Gravel gardens slowly lose their effectiveness over time as humus and fine particles collect between the stones, so the layer will need to be renewed or added to on a regular basis.

Even under the shade of trees you can do something to help self-seeding plants such as *Galanthus* species (snowdrops), *Eranthis hyemalis* (winter aconites) and *Anemone nemorosa* (wood anemones) thrive. They are inhibited by ground-covering plants and large piles of slowly decomposing leaves, so avoid planting shaded areas thickly with ground cover and try reducing piles of autumn leaves with the lawn mower so that they can decompose quickly. Repeat and plant a few of the above-listed plants. You will be surprised how quickly these early spring flowers establish themselves.

On Sweden's east coast, bales of white peat are used to make raised beds that have survived for decades. They quickly become covered in moss when the relative humidity is sufficiently high. The beds are then populated by other plants that tolerate low pH levels.

Raising soil pH

Some specialist plants thrive in soils with a pH value of 6.5 and higher, especially plants from regions where the soil has a high lime content. These aren't lime-loving plants per se, but rather plants that are able to tolerate these conditions. Flora that spontaneously populate such sites thrived in cities after World War II, growing in piles of rubble containing slowly disintegrating mortar, stucco and plaster of lime and cement.

In gardens where soils with high amounts of organic matter have developed over years, the soil pH is usually far below 6.5. To raise the pH, you can work construction rubble, lime grit, or, in coastal regions, mussel shells into the ground. Mussel shells can be difficult to buy in large quantities but can be collected simply by walking along the beach. Crushed eggshells can be effective for a small-scale project, but if you want to

significantly raise the pH of the soil, you'll need to be an enthusiastic eater of eggs.

The most straightforward soil amendment for raising pH is probably agricultural lime acquired from a garden centre. Its main effective ingredient is calcium carbonate ($CaCO_3$), though there are other components as well. The amount of dolomite in the source material will dictate the amount of magnesium contained in it. Rock flour also contains calcium carbonate and is available from specialist suppliers. Whatever product you choose, be aware that the soil pH can only be raised in the long term through regular, repeated application.

Because of its caustic effects, it is strongly recommended that you do not use quicklime (CaO).

If you have access to a lot of decaying wood, try populating it with *Anemone blanda* (winter windflower). Make a wood pile with the most decayed wood on top, then insert some bulbs and cover them with moss. Provided the wood pile is kept moist enough during spring, a spectacular display of flowers will develop within a few years.

Lowering soil pH

There are plants that prefer acid conditions, but it can be difficult to maintain these soil conditions in the long term. Additionally, as the soil pH drops below 5, toxic aluminium ions and heavy metals are released that can lead to growth problems for many species. Some plants can only survive in these conditions in symbiotic relationships with fungi.

Many highly competitive species can survive in acidic soils while at the same time certain acids inhibit germination. A few decades ago when acid rain commonly fell it was easy to maintain acidic conditions but today it is a challenge to keep soil pH levels low for the long haul. For this reason, simply buying an acidic substrate is not enough and you will need to consider site conditions and other influences.

Peat moss is the most convenient material for lowering soil pH to create bog gardens. Not all peat is the same, though: most peat moss products from garden centres are enriched with fertilizers and have been chopped up. White peat is a better option because it is less processed, lower in nutrients, and more likely to contain viable spores and seeds.

Bog gardens are established in much the same way as garden ponds in scale and construction, with a waterproof membrane as a liner. Soak the peat first, then lay it to create a convex surface. Lay upside-down pots and buckets with holes in them at the bottom of the bed to reduce the amount of peat required.

Another option for acidifying the soil is the regular application of needle litter from conifers. Take care not to completely cover the ground with needles as this would make germination impossible. Instead, cover only part of the ground or work the needles into the soil with a spade or hoe. As the needles decompose, growth-inhibiting chemicals are often released. Plants can overcome these with the help of mycorrhizal fungi, which can be inoculated into the soil beforehand.

In general, establishing self-seeding plants in acid soils is something for the more experienced gardener. Keep in mind too that the extraction of peat is highly damaging to the ecology of peat bogs and should be viewed with scepticism.

Further possibilities for transforming your soil

Light, sandy soils can be made somewhat heavier with the addition of clay, while heavy soils can be lightened by incorporating sand, grit and/or compost. Even salt, typically thought of as being plant-unfriendly, can be used in moderation in small spaces. A large number of self-seeding plants are found on beaches and other coastal areas, and along the edges of roads that are treated with salt in winter. To prevent salt from leaching out of your soil and damaging surrounding areas, use a waterproof membrane as for a bog garden.

Gardening from the bottom up

When gardening with self-seeding plants, you need to approach the planning of beds and paths in a slightly different way. It's not about whether a plant grows in visual harmony with its neighbour or which plants should be positioned towards the front or the rear of the bed. Instead, the main consideration is the type of plants that should grow in a particular area of the garden. By establishing new sites or enhancing the characteristics of existing sites, you can make precisely the right conditions for a wide range plants, sometimes to the mystification of your garden visitors.

On first sight, a newly landscaped garden for self-seeders appears to offer just one homogeneous environment, but with underground profiling you can create very different growth conditions that over time yield surprisingly diverse results.

To achieve this, excavate areas that are to remain vegetation-free or serve as paths to a depth of at least 20 cm (8 in) – the deeper they are, the longer they last. At the same time, make these paths at least 1m (3¼ ft) wide as bordering plants often encroach on paths. Areas where tap-rooted plants are to grow should be dug to a depth of 10–15 cm (4–6 in). Establishing gravel beds in this way can be especially appealing. To adapt existing beds, carefully remove 3–5 cm (1–2 in) of soil then replace with gravel or grit.

Gravel surfaces that are to remain vegetation-free should be made sufficiently wide and deep. Plants will stay away, seemingly by magic, in an otherwise uniform-appearing bed.

Miles of path-like strips of gravel 1 m (3¼ ft) deep are found at Dungeness. This concept can easily be used in the garden as gravel paths hardly require any maintenance.

Het Vlackeland – Swift-blooming splendour

opposite:
Species-rich, well-balanced compositions of short-lived plants like this one require much knowledge and care. *Anethum graveolens* (dill) grows in the foreground, while *Verbascum* species (mullein) and *Atriplex hortensis* var. *rubra* (red orach) stand tall behind.

left:
Once established, *Verbena hastata* (verbena) becomes a reliable member of a dynamic, well-tended garden.

In 2003, landscape designer Madelien van Hasselt and her partner Willy Oorthuijsen purchased a 8700 m² (2.15 acre) parcel of land in the province of Zeeland in the Netherlands. For the design of open expanses and borders, she drew inspiration from the surrounding apple orchards: straight-lined and clearly defined. An experienced designer, she was confident that the plants would later introduce a diversity of shapes. To achieve results as quickly as possible, she first sowed the seed of numerous annuals and short-lived perennials. Over time, more and more perennials were added. The fact that so many species from the original seed-sowing still play such a prominent role in the garden is largely due to the fact that a wider range of conditions for regeneration that were provided for the plants. The success of the garden is also because Madelien von Hasselt treasures such dynamic splendour and knows how to use it to her advantage. Her garden is a spectacular example of the breathtaking effect self-seeding plants can achieve in a short period of time, and of the diversity that can be maintained.

In July, little of the original form of the garden is recognizable. The awns of *Hordeum jubatum* (annual foxtail barley) reach into the middle of the garden paths and are met by *Centranthus ruber* (red valerian) growing from the other side. In the foreground is long-lasting *Nepeta* 'Six Hills Giant' (catnip); as it is a hybrid, it does not self-seed. To ensure that garden paths are accessible for walking along, even in summer, they must be at least 2 m (6½ ft) wide.

Nassella tenuissima (Mexican feather grass) forms a thin matrix through which the midsummer-blooming *Kniphofia* 'Little Maid' (red-hot poker) and *Verbena bonariensis* (Argentinian vervain) protrude. In these proportions, all the plants are equally visible. However, after several hard winters, this planting no longer exists. Van Hasselt sees the positive side of this: setbacks provide space for new plant combinations, an important concept when gardening with self-seeding plants.

This area of the garden is a beautiful
spectacle in the low-angled light
of early summer evenings. *Knautia
macedonica* (Macedonian scabious),
Papaver rhoeas (red poppy), a red
variety of *P. somniferum* (opium poppy,
left border of the photograph) and
a few *Atriplex hortensis* var. *rubra*
(red orach) provide the red hues.
Gold and silver come from a stand of
Stipa gigantea (golden oats), *Nassella
tenuissima* (Mexican feather grass),
Deschampsia cespitosa (tufted hair
grass, background) and *Hordeum
jubatum* (foxtail barley, foreground).
The seedheads of *Allium aflatunense*
(flowering onion), which blooms in
late spring, can remain standing until
autumn, when they develop interesting
contours.

In August, the flowers of *Telekia speciosa* (heart-leaved ox-eye) and *Verbascum nigrum* (black mullein) slowly fade but the borders maintain interest with late-flowering dahlias.

A simple combination that works for months is that of *Crocosmia* 'Lucifer' (montbretia), *Nigella damascena* (love-in-a-mist) and *Deschampsia cespitosa* (tufted hair grass). In the square of meadow in the background, *Dipsacus fullonum* (Fuller's teasel) appears almost sculptural and will stand well into the following year.

Foeniculum vulgare 'Giant Bronze' (bronze fennel) and *Verbascum nigrum* (black mullein) make a vibrant combination, emphasized by the dark stalks of *Verbena hastata* (verbena).

This is a beautiful example of how self-seeding plants – in this case *Deschampsia cespitosa* (tufted hair grass) and *Telekia speciosa* (heart-leaved ox-eye) – can surround long-lived species such as *Ligularia dentata* (leopard plant), *Crocosmia* 'Emberglow' and *C.* 'Lucifer' (montbretia). Similarities as well as differences in flower and leaf shape can contribute to harmonious and exhilarating plant combinations.

Thanks to its dense vegetation, the grid-like arrangement of the garden is hardly visible in summer. The design of the garden can be seen only where wide paths or large lawns meet up with beds. The horizontal lines of the hedges and canopy road, which lie outside the borders of the property, give the garden the enclosure it needs. In the foreground, *Hordeum jubatum* (foxtail barley) forms a thin carpet, through which annuals (*Papaver rhoeas*, *Verbena bonariensis*) and longer-lived plants such as *Agapanthus* (African lily) and *Liatris spicata* (button snakewort) grow. Around the pond, several *Lythrum salicaria* (purple loosestrife) plants have set seed.

In contemporary garden design, pastels and earth tones are often preferred and mixed colours and yellows are avoided but beds with several short-living plants appears to offer an alternative. Carefully considered quantities of reddish leaves and stems give depth to this planting despite the melange of different species. Among the plants used are *Linaria purpurea* (purple toadflax, foreground), *Silene coronaria* (rose campion), *Centranthus ruber* (red valerian), *Atriplex hortensis* var. *rubra* (red orach), *Salvia sclarea* (clary sage), *Oenothera glazioviana* (red-sepal evening primrose) and *Pastinaca sativa* (wild parsnip). Although Madelien van Hasselt loves to experiment, she is happy to use well-known plants when they have proven to be healthy and robust.

In the front garden, raised beds have been made by using timber for the structure and backfilling with humus-rich soil. Dense vegetation has since developed that offers little space for seeds to germinate and establish. Paths laid with mussel shells suit the natural, informal appearance of the garden.

A   *Knautia macedonica* (Macedonian scabious)
B   *Gypsophila repens* (creeping gypsophila)
C   *Salvia nemorosa* (Balkan clary, from seed)
D   *Salvia nemorosa* 'Caradonna' (Balkan clary)
E   *Reseda alba* (white mignonette)
F   *Sedum* (stonecrop, from seed)
G   *Helleborus argutifolius* (holly-leaved hellebore, from seed)
H   *Marrubium incanum* (horehound)
J   *Salvia × sylvestris* 'Blauhügel' (wood sage)

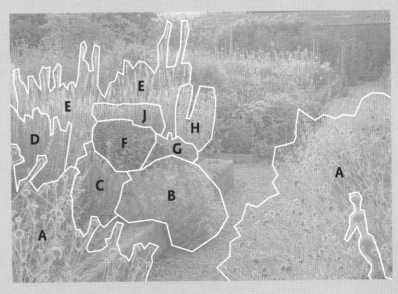

Here, *Centranthus ruber* (red valerian) and *Knautia macedonica* (Macedonian scabious) have set seed in the mussel shell path.

Annuals and short-lived perennials thrive splendidly not just within raised beds but also along their edges, as these *Alcea rosea* (hollyhocks) and *Calendula officinalis* (marigolds) show. *Allium* 'Globemaster' and *Stachys byzantina* (lamb's tongue) combine to make the massive timbers appear less formal.

STRATEGIES FOR DESIGN AND MAINTENANCE

Gardens with self-seeding plants constantly change their appearance; surprises are integral to the concept. Small shifts in maintenance of the garden can result in dramatic changes in how it looks. This means you need to carefully consider how to proceed in the garden in order to give it a chance to succeed.

Can self-seeding plants be controlled?

Self-seeding plants may at first seem hard to manage as their intrinsic waywardness means that the garden is in constant flux. Creating permanent groupings of them is out of the question as their random dispersal thwarts all attempts at order – an important component of design. Yet it is precisely these aspects that make gardening with self-seeding plants so alluring. The tendency to change encourages experimentation and leaves room for making mistakes – if there are such things in this context – which quickly disappear. It is this blend of curiosity and coincidence that has such potential for achieving new results, something that is easy to forget when you focus on the standard rules of garden design.

Self-seeding plants make it easy for us by simply demonstrating through seed dispersal the quantities and proportions that are appropriate for each species. Disregarding the information plants give us can have dire consequences. At the same time, the garden is not the same as a wild landcape and we humans also have needs that we are trying to fulfil when we lay out a garden. We cannot rely on simply replacing design plans with careful maintenance of the plant balance. As well as selecting sites where self-seeding plants are allowed to proliferate, contrasts need to be created throughout the garden to provide tension, balance and emphasis. Clearly defined architectural forms and areas of quiet that are the result of traditional garden planning provide these.

Unwanted plants

Could self-seeding gardens pose a threat? Environmentalists would say yes, that invasive non-native plants that establish themselves and pose a threat to the continued existence of local plants are indeed a threat. Yet when you consider how many plants of exotic origin grow in our gardens, the actual number of these that have managed to escape beyond the garden fence is astonishingly few. Even smaller is the number of those that are truly a danger to indigenous plants and even these aliens tend not to be problematic everywhere, just in sensitive environments where protected, competitively weak species prevail.

It is often difficult to tell if a plant is potentially dangerous or not. Even today's most unwanted invasive plants were not obviously dangerous in the beginning. Indeed, any species that propagates itself in new environments by seed (generatively) or via runners (vegetatively) could be viewed with suspicion. This would include all non-indigenous plants useful for the self-seeding garden.

So what does this mean for this type of gardening? One pragmatic approach would be to estimate the actual risks involved. Is there a conservation area nearby? Are there areas in the immediate vicinity that self-seeding plants could use as a springboard into the wilderness? Are there ecological corridors such as streets, railways or running water that plants could exploit to spread beyond their immediate surroundings?

By choosing suitable conditions, it is possible to limit some plants to certain spots in the garden. In the crevices of these distinctive steps at Great Dixter, *Erigeron karvinskianus* (Mexican fleabane) and *Centranthus ruber* (red valerian) thrive. They love locations that are dry, especially in winter.

The greatest practical problem is that you might lose interest in a particular species and face the challenge of removing plants from the garden once they have firmly established themselves. This may not sound much to those with no experience with self-seeding plants, but if you have ambitious design goals, one wrongly coloured flower or too strongly dominating species can be a thorn in your side.

The simplest way to remove self-seeding plants is to reduce the amount of surface area available for their seeds to germinate. Unfortunately, this also inhibits any other species that might need the same space for germination. Besides, it is all but impossible to identify every spot where a seed could potentially germinate.

The most effective way to eliminate a "*planta non grata*" from the home garden is to consistently pull out the plants just before or just when they begin to flower. Weeding at this stage has the advantage that the plant will be at a point in its life cycle where it will be easy to identify. If you are more confident with plant identification, you can also pull out seedlings immediately after germination, when they will provide little resistance. However, since most seeds are viable for many years, it will probably be a long time before the area is clear of the plants you want to eliminate.

Impatiens glandulifera (Himalayan balsam) was first introduced as an ornamental, but quickly escaped the garden and is today a feared invasive plant that has spread along many rivers and streams. When using self-seeding plants, you should always be aware of their potential dangers and keep plants listed on internet sites such as nobanis.org, europe-aliens.org, and plants.usda.gov out of your garden.

The compost heap

From an ecological point of view, composting your own biodegradable waste is of course a good thing. However, most home compost heaps (or at least their outer layers) rarely reach the 70–80°C (158–176°F) required to destroy the viability of seeds. Later, when you spread your compost on the garden, seeds are reintroduced at a time when growing conditions are optimal. This is great if the seeds happen to be of desirable species, but if they are of weeds you have painstakingly pulled out you have unwittingly created more work for yourself.

Few compost heaps are as beautiful as those at Great Dixter. The growth of *Dipsacus fullonum* (common teasel), *Leucanthemum vulgare* (ox-eye daisy) and *Papaver somniferum* (opium poppy), however, makes clear how many seeds potentially ride the compost train back into the garden.

Every picture needs a frame

Only when our needs for safety and familiarity are met are we open to the urge to seek out the unknown and possible danger. This is anchored deep in our subconscious and is relevant to our perception of gardens and plants. When we enter a room that we don't already know, we seek to orient ourselves with familiar elements, such as geometric shapes, straight lines and right angles. These help to assure us that things are as they should be and allow us to feel more at ease. In themselves, though, these elements are fairly boring and tend not to inspire closer inspection.

Another important aspect is that our eyes regularly seek out reference points, then return to exploration. These "resting" sites are mostly found in uniform, monotone surfaces. The colour green has a well-known calming effect, but other, darker hues are also restful.

Translated to the garden, this means designing frames for areas to be dominated by self-seeding plants, making appropriate "stage scenery" of hedges, walls and objects (glass, plastic, metal) and creating a serene backdrop. There is no necessity for lawns, though beyond a certain garden size it becomes increasingly difficult to create pleasant contrasts of uniform colours using only hedges and walls. The light green colour is another aspect in favour of the lawn, as it lends a bit of freshness to the garden in autumn and winter, where otherwise the brown hues of dead vegetation prevail.

Trimmed hedges and lawns—such as here at Le Jardin Plume in France – provide superb contrast of form, enhancing the whole garden. Here, *Inula magnifica* and *Oenothera odorata* (evening primrose) grow beside yew hedges.

At Le Jardin Plume, meadow-like areas are framed by mown grass – as simple as it is effective.

The Dutch Wave gardeners

Until just a few years ago, seed stalks and dead plant material attracted little aesthetic appreciation. "Proper" horticultural practice called for the removal of anything that was no longer flowering. In the 1980s, a group of Dutch gardeners and landscape designers – including figures who have become well-known today, such as Piet Oudolf and Henk Gerritsen – began proclaiming the beauty of dried vegetation and cultivating plants that had until then been regarded as uninteresting. The chic brown and black hues of their plantings are set in clearly defined spatial arrangements and surrounded with hedges and other design elements. Species that possess a strong inherent structure contribute particularly well in this context over a long period. Of all the Dutch Wave gardeners, only Ton ter Linden practises another approach.

It is especially important to have strong, permanent structures to provide a framework as the vegetation goes into dormancy. Piet Oudolf, whose style has become more and more naturalistic over time, has used many different plants to form the hedges that balance his landscapes of flowering perennials and grasses.

Despite his 78 years, Ton ter Linden pursues his twin passions for painting and garden design with vigour. He is convinced that his extravagant style of gardening is what keeps him fit.

Ton ter Linden – chaotic charm in the garden

The idea that painters see their gardens first and foremost as outdoor studios and sources of inspiration has been familiar ever since the time of Claude Monet. This combination of artistic and horticultural activity is strikingly evident in the Dutchman Ton ter Linden, who attracted international attention with his first garden in Ruinen, Netherlands. His sophisticated combination plantings arranged in separate, colour co-ordinated garden "rooms" were particularly highly regarded. Although they were the result of carefully considered design, they had a naturalness that was altogether new.

In his third garden, in Friesland, he has managed to create exciting effects as before, but ones that change on a daily basis. Shrubs, flowering perennials, grasses, bulbs and annuals are grown in combinations based on colour, shape, and especially atmosphere and ambience. Self-seeding plants have been an important element of Linden's gardens for many years and he edits them through removal and transplanting. In this way he has been able to realize his gardening vision without losing its natural charm and individuality.

Armed with an asparagus knife for removing weeds and loosening the soil, Linden roams about his beds, re-establishing order and making space for new growth. "You should never have the impression that you are working in your garden. It should look as if Mother Nature herself is the artist," is his motto. However, this method of gardening is definitely labour intensive, with the majority of tasks being done by hand. Synthetic fertilizers and chemical herbicides and pesticides are anathema, and the constant state of change in the garden requires almost daily intervention. Nevertheless, Linden sees striving for a balance between culture and nature as an ongoing creative challenge and a fascinating adventure. Maybe that's why he does not look 78 years of age.

The spring garden reveals a colour-coordinated composition of *Aquilegia* (columbine) and *Allium* species (flowering alliums) that Linden developed the previous year from seedlings.

A simple trick for populating gaps between paving is to place container-grown plants in the area and let them set seed. You can then move the container around to disperse the seeds more widely.

Paved surfaces, such as this terrace in Great Dixter, look charming with plants growing between the gaps. Species that are often too invasive in a border, such as *Alchemilla mollis* (lady's mantle) and *Leucanthemum vulgare* (ox-eye daisy), can be kept under control here. Simply cutting back after flowering will suffice.

Plants in crevices and joints

Self-seeding plants look in their element in the crevices and gaps that emerge in hard landscaping and nowhere are they more fascinating, thriving in a site where there is scarcely any soil or water. Yet it is precisely these sites that offer some plants exactly what they need to thrive – the protection from strong competitors. Once established, their roots can penetrate so deeply that they are able to reach nutrients and water that are invisible at the surface. So how can we get plants to grow here?

Horizontal surfaces

Cobbled or paved surfaces where the gaps are to be populated by plants need to be made wide enough to accommodate both plantings and foot traffic. Self-seeding plants are able to thrive where there is no real planting medium so every place where the ground meets paths, walls or hedges, there is a joint of some kind that can be enriched with plants. These areas may be individually small, but the overall results can be remarkable.

Where there are small paving slabs or bricks, joints take up a comparatively large proportion of the surface area, which means that there is more potential space for plants to establish. This could potentially lead to paths becoming obscured by vegetation. Larger flagstones can offer an even better solution, though the trade-off may be poorer penetration of water into the soil.

In principle, any paved area that allows for the accumulation of humus or the penetration of roots into deeper soil layers should work. Newer paths built to conform to building standards are designed to prevent these things, as humus does not provide long-term stability. Fortunately, few things are built as perfectly as they are designed. Wherever moss or weeds start to grow in the joints, populating them with other, more desirable plants should also be possible.

First, remove all weeds and loosen whatever substrate there is within the joints with a knife. See the following for options for greening crevices and joints:

— The simplest option is sowing seed. Make sure the joints are kept consistently moist until germination.
— Because of the minimal space available, planting out plug plants is more difficult and requires sufficiently wide joints. First clean out the joint as much as possible and free the roots of your plant from the potting compost. Then place the plant roots in the joint – a knife or spatula may be helpful here. Finally, pack as much soil as possible back into the joint.
— A very simple option, though not always achievable, is the removal of a paver from the path so that you can set a plant in the gap.
— Putting a plant in a pot at the site until it sets and drops seed can be highly effective. Another advantage of this method is that the plant can be used at different sites over time.

Vertical surfaces

Greening walls with plants is viewed with scepticism by some due to concern that the plants may ruin the structure. This worry is usually unfounded as hardly any annuals or herbaceous perennials have roots capable of causing the kind of damage woody plants cause. Besides, plants do not grow into perfectly mortared walls because they cannot survive the lack of water and high pH levels. This can change over the decades, of course, as the pH of the mortar falls and/or moisture makes its way into the masonry.

Dry-stone walls – that is, walls built without mortar – are more appropriate for plants, especially when they support a slope and are backfilled with soil. The same is true for walls as for paved paths: wherever weeds grow, desirable plants should be able to grow there too. As populating a vertical site can be more difficult than a horizontal one, here are a few tips:

— Seed can be used in walls, too. Mix soil, seeds and water into a thick mud and use this to fill a cake icing bag or large syringe. Press the mud as deep into the joints as possible. In the days and weeks that follow, it can be a challenge to keep the seeds wet without washing out the joints. The best tool here is a fog machine, though these are rarely found in a domestic setting. Alternatively, a spray gun or a lawn sprinkler falling just short of the wall could both work.

— Plug plants can only be established with great skill. The best place to plant would be a large joint, though keep in mind that you should never remove a stone for better planting as this would compromise the structural integrity of the wall. Younger plants are most successful, as they recover from the transplanting process better than older ones.

— Planting at the base of the wall is easier than within it. Gravity makes no exception for seeds and many low-blooming plants could take decades to populate the upper reaches of the wall. However, the seeds of some species, such as *Pseudofumaria lutea* (yellow corydalis) are carried upwards by ants.

— Wherever possible, ensure that seed falls onto the wall from above. Where walls intercept a downward slope, planting above the coping (top) of the wall is ideal. For freestanding walls, use the potted plant trick described above. Here it is important to ensure that the pot is securely fastened to the wall coping.

Well-laid dry-stone walls of limestone can be richly furnished with plants. *Centranthus ruber* (valerian), seen here as the white variety 'Albus', and *Erigeron karvinskianus* (Mexican fleabane) make this wall in Great Dixter appear less substantial than it actually is.

Crushed limestone beds

Not all limestone is the same – at least, as far as choosing the right material for a crushed limestone bed is concerned. Be sure to use soft limestone that dissolves more completely so that the intended pH level of the bed is established immediately. Additionally, a high proportion of fines – limestone crushed to a fine powder – makes for a better seed bed. If you are unsure, do a hand test: take some lightly wetted gravel in your hand and scrunch it around. If a crust starts to form on your hand, this means the lime is dusting off and the material is appropriate. For ecological as well as aesthetic reasons, source local if possible. As there was no local option for the example described here, we used "Yellow Sun" with a granulation of 8–16 mm from southern France.

After choosing an appropriate location with full sun, remove the topsoil to the depth of a spade (about 25 cm/10 in). This will require great care if tap-rooted weeds are present. Depending on the quality of the soil or subsoil, fill the bottom of the bed with an appropriate substrate mixture to a depth of 15 cm (6 in). If the soil is clay, shingle or highly compacted, use a 1:1 mixture of compost/humus-rich garden soil and sand. For sandy soil, as shown here, use a 3:1 mixture of compost/humus-rich garden soil and bentonite to soak up and hold water and nutrients.

Bentonite bought in the form of cat litter is economically priced. Use only untreated bentonite, which is easily identified by dropping a few grains into a glass of water and stirring. Within a minute, untreated bentonite will have completely dissolved.

To save yourself work, mix the substrate on site, alternating between ingredients as you add them to the soil. Work with bentonite only in dry conditions to avoid it forming clumps. Level the substrate and compact it with a lawn roller before bringing in the crushed limestone.

For a depth of 10 cm (4 in), you will need about 150 kg (330 lb) crushed limestone per square metre (10¾ sq ft). After levelling and lightly tamping the limestone you can begin planting.

To help plants grow faster and adapt to the site, wash the potting soil from the roots of plants in pots. Water after planting and in the days that follow. For best results, leave at least 50 cm (20 in) between plants and garden paths.

The following year, add another 25 kg (55 lb) of crushed limestone per square metre (10¾ sq ft), taking care not to damage your plants. Mid-spring is a good time, as all the plants should have sprouted but will still be relatively small. Covering them with pots helps to protect them while you add the limestone.

Sowing seed directly into a virgin crushed limestone bed risks the seed being washed so far below the surface that the developing seedlings don't get enough light to survive. To prevent this, spread bentonite or clay soil on a few spots in the bed, water, and plant seed in these "islands". Later, as dust and soil brought in by the wind slowly accumulates in the bed, creating islands will no longer be necessary.

Meadows – cultivating chaos on a grand scale

A flowering meadow is the sign of a thriving ecosystem that can inspire onlookers with a longing for unspoilt fields and mountain pastures full of native plants. For years, seed producers have been trying to sell a small slice of this idyll in the form of a seed packet, and the results are often disappointing. This is not always the fault of the seed companies; the fact is that it is difficult to create a successful meadow in a small plot behind a terraced house.

With a few exceptions, meadows are managed environments that are primarily dedicated to hay production. High hay yields can be achieved by using new grass varieties and the application of large amounts of fertilizer that also suppresses herbaceous perennials and other flowering plants. These days, the only meadows that reliably produce large amounts of flowers are dry grasslands and low-nutrient or calcareous grasslands, where gaps between the individual grass plants allow room for herbaceous perennials to germinate and grow. To maintain calcareous grasslands, grass cuttings need to be consistently removed for years, if not decades, and the overall influx of nutrients needs to be held back.

To achieve this, you can work with parasitic plants that weaken grasses such as *Rhinanthus* species (rattles), though seeds may be hard to come by as they do not store well. Ideally, use fresh hay from a nearby meadow to "inoculate" your meadow with seed. Local environmental organizations can also help you with suppliers.

In recent years, renowned landscape designers have come to appreciate the meadow – or more accurately, the principle of the meadow – and use it in their own work. They are aware that one of the benefits of a meadow is that it is easy to establish and maintain. Some have supplemented the grasses with highly competitive perennials to increase the number of flowers, but although these plantings look attractive they leave little room for self-seeding and dynamism. More promising is a type of gravel turf surface on which a humus-poor, coarse substrate such as pea gravel is laid and planted with dry grassland species. Though it may look meagre for the first few years, that soon changes and in later years the gardener needs to take measures to prevent too much humus from building up and too much grass from establishing.

Great Dixter's meadows are seen by many visitors who enjoy plants in flower from early spring through to summer. The maintenance regime includes regular mowing and suppression of grasses using the *Rhinanthus* species (rattles) that colonize and steal nutrients from the roots of neighbouring grasses.

Mulleins (here *Verbascum chaixii* and its white strain 'Album')
are some of the easiest self-seeding plants to grow, though they
require a lot of space that other plants could use. For this reason,
keep an eye out for their characteristic leaf rosettes. If you find
any, ask yourself: "Do I really want another mullein plant here?"
Often you can achieve a dramatic effect with just a few plants.

Managing the mix

The Austrian conductor Herbert von Karajan once said that the key to his profession was to know how to avoid distracting the orchestra. If you imagine yourself as conductor of your garden, try at first just to get a sense of who is performing and what composition is being played.

Don't worry, you will soon find the melody. The important thing is always to listen (or rather look) carefully. Among self-seeding plants you will find diverse characters whose idiosyncrasies need to be considered when caring for the garden.

Free bloomers

These are mostly annuals (but sometimes biennials and short-lived perennials) that produce relatively few leaves but many small flowers. For them to develop to their fullest potential, they need to be present in large numbers since individual plants are easily lost due to their weak structure. After dropping seed, these plants can be drastically reduced in number as they seldom offer attractive textures that are worth keeping after flowering.

By interspersing different species, you increase the interest of the garden but take care – combining too many species or distributing them evenly in the garden can ruin the natural effect.

Magnificence

This characteristic is often found in biennial and monocarpic plants. Magnificent plants first collect their energy in storage organs and grow large leaf rosettes, then, in the year of flowering, they send up sturdy stalks. Distinct from the solitary plants of classical perennial plantings, they are relatively light and informal despite the fact that they sometimes grow taller than the average person.

These plants look most impressive when used singly with their own space around them, especially in locations where one would not expect to find such a plant. They often have a very bold structure that it is worth keeping through winter.

Be aware, however, that their dominance can detract from other plants and even suppress their growth. Their large rosettes often inhibit the seeds of other species from germinating. Selectively pruning them for the benefit of their neighbours, however, is not the thing to do, as these magnificent plants need their own space to appear at their best.

Gap-finders

This is perhaps the most typical kind of self-seeding plant. They appear to come from nowhere, build up an obvious structure and flower prolifically. No matter if they are annual or perennial, individual or in groups, they are welcome additions and do not disturb other plants. Gap-finders are some of the most vibrant elements of any garden. Let them be, unless they happen to be of a colour that doesn't go with their surroundings. They are less pretty when carrying fruit, which can be removed to improve the overall appearance of the garden.

Salt of the earth

These are mostly perennial plants, but unlike species typically found in perennial plantings, they give the impression – through the continual sprouting of individual plants into thick tufts and clumps – that they've always been here. Remove plants only if you fear they may dominate the entire garden or suppress other species, which rarely happens. More often, your concern will be protecting their slow-growing seedlings from the surrounding vegetation.

Fritillaria meleagris (snake's head fritillary) is a gap-finder that never becomes a nuisance. Here they have seeded themselves in the middle of a carpet of *Hakonechloa macra* (Japanese forest grass). While the grass is dormant, the snake's head fritillary gets ahead to take advantage of the conditions.

When gardening with self-seeding plants, find time to observe them and look for solutions to the questions that arise, such as: how long should you resist something that goes against your original ideas; can unforeseen yet interesting developments be accentuated; and what happens when the things you see in the garden one day are gone the next.

You can also implement ideas you might know from designing traditional gardens, such as creating colour schemes and flows, repetition, enhancement, lines of sight, vertical separations and so on. But you might start questioning whether it is really interesting to limit yourself and the garden to this standard repertoire. Either way, keep in mind that gardens need a basic level of order and structure to be accepted as a garden by many. They also need both open spaces as well as areas that create intimacy and protection.

Three tips for creative gardeners

— Allow self-seeding plants onto patches that are not normally reserved for plants, such as masonry joints, gravel paths and driveways, and the "clean" strips of ground that border the house. In this way, the garden develops a lively, informal character.
— Less is more! Patches where one species blooms en masse, coupled with another to give structure, are especially spectacular.
— Enjoy peak flowering times while still thinking one step ahead. The more diversity to be found in a given patch, the more systematically you will have to observe individual species and "free" them as necessary. Large-leaved plants such as *Verbascum* and *Digitalis* have a tendency to suffocate their neighbours.

In Henrik Zetterlund's garden in Sweden, seed of *Paeonia obovata* (obovate peony), a species from China, was sown six years ago from a plant that was already growing here. Without further human intervention, several handsome examples now stand in the garden.

101

Picking your time

When you garden with self-seeding plants, there are no rules about what to do when. Plants can be removed practically any time. Nevertheless, it makes sense to pursue a few goals during certain growth phases.

The seedling phase

Plants are easiest to pull out during this stage – in fact it often suffices to crush the cotyledons or cover them with a layer of soil or grit. Still, this only makes sense if you know what you're trying to achieve or are definite that you do not want any plants in a certain spot. Seedlings can be difficult to recognize unless you're prepared to go through the garden with a magnifying glass.

The growth phase

At this point, plants display their characteristic foliage and growth habit, so the trained eye can spot individual plants that are out of place and remove them. If you'd like colourful leaves or variegated shapes in your garden, now is the time to remove green-leaved variants. Equally, if you'd like to keep compact plants, remove the giants.

Slugs – the enemy of the self-sown garden

The Nepalese proverb "He who embraces his enemy, renders him immobile" may contain much wisdom, but from the point of view of trying to control the biggest problem of almost any garden, it's not helpful. Slugs, especially *Arion vulgaris*, the Spanish slug, are connoisseurs of crisp, fresh seedlings. Even plants that later develop effective forms of defence against slugs are vulnerable as seedlings, and what's particularly unfortunate is that when you're working with self-seeding plants you often don't even know what's been eaten.

Even if you have yet to find slugs in your garden, it is an absolute must to take preventative measures against them. The most effective seems to be spreading slug and snail bait granules in early spring. Metaldehyde and ferric phosphate-based compounds are supposedly environmentally friendly, the latter more so than the former.

Simply collecting and removing slugs from the garden can be very effective, albeit time-consuming. The important thing is to always be one step ahead.

Campanula persicifolia
(bellflower)

Eryngium giganteum
(Miss Willmott's ghost)

Centranthus ruber
(red valerian)

Onopordum acanthium
(cotton thistle)

Salvia nemorosa
(Balkan clary)

Helleborus argutifolius
(holly-leaved hellebore)

Hieracium maculatum
(spotted hawkweed)

Verbena hastata
(blue vervain)

Telekia speciosa
(heart-leaf oxeye)

103

Verbena bonariensis (verbena), with its dark stalks, has a graphic quality, especially when planted close to light-coloured plants as they are here behind *Nigella damascena* (love-in-a-mist). Verbena has little leaf mass so you can let stands become dense.

In late summer, verbena is irresistible with its flowers blooming for weeks. Can we ever get enough? Yes, more quickly than we might imagine. If it grows in too many patches, the contours of other plants are lost and there is too much of the same thing.

The start of flowering

Removing colour variants is the way to achieve a certain uniformity of colour within patches of species or strains that have a lot of variation. Many hitherto inconspicuous plants may suddenly become very dominant once they are flowering, and reducing them can help retain a sense of balance.

During flowering

This is the time for finishing touches – the removal of individual plants. The best strategy for this is to take morning walks through the garden that end at the compost heap. By removing flower stalks (but not the leaf rosette near the ground) of biennials, monocarpic plants and short-lived perennials, you can often delay their blooming period, and thus their dying off, by months or even several years. When this is performed regularly in a section of the planting, fresh seed develops again and again. Soon, plants of the same species at different stages of development will live side by side. You can avoid flowerless years in this way, especially for biennials and monocarpic plants.

Selecting variations

Sometimes desirable colours or forms appear within a species and to maintain these, they need to be selected, saved and propagated. Genetically identical plants (those that are produced from dividing plants or cuttings) that have these traits, along with plants that produce viable seed that yields true-to-type offspring, are called varieties. You can also select seed of a certain variety for several generations until nearly all progeny display the trait you have been selecting for. This is a strain of the variety.

In a garden on the island of Bornholm, Sweden, *Foeniculum vulgare* (fennel) is cut back before blooming to maintain its leaves for longer. Pruning stimulates new sprouting, turning fennel into a dense, feathery leaved shrub.

The end of flowering

By now it will be clear which plants you have in the garden and you can decide whether you still want them or not. By reducing the number of plants at this point you can plan the next blooming period most effectively. Species that produce seed very vigorously should generally be dug out at the end of flowering – a few individual plants are plenty for establishing the next generation. There is also the option of pruning many short-lived species (including some biennials) to stimulate a second blooming in late summer or autumn.

The stalks of *Telekia speciosa* (heart-leaf oxeye) are highly decorative and remain sturdy for a long time. The plant produces seed in reasonable quantities.

After dropping seed

Now is the time to remove all dead vegetation, including plant parts or entire plants, that doesn't offer any attractive structure, texture or colour. Skilful work is required to ensure the garden still looks beautiful for a time as plants gradually decay and then die. There's no need to be too concerned about mistakes, though, as the garden can be easily be guided back to how you want it.

The garden should be cleaned up at the end of winter to find space for new seedlings to establish. This means removing those last few dead plants from the soil.

Resettlement

Mother Nature is not infallible – at least not when it comes to our creative ideas. Sometimes a plant is in the wrong place by just a few centimetres or a flower colour doesn't fit with our desired colour flow. In this situation, it's always worth thinking about where else you could use it rather than just adding it to the compost heap. Plants are best able to cope with transplanting when they are still very small (tap-rooted plants can only be transplanted at this point). Make sure you offer them a suitable site; do not, for example, transplant sunlovers into the shade.

Foeniculum vulgare (fennel) is beautiful even without its delicate leaves and, with this coating of frost, looks dramatic in winter.

The only constant is change

Even if you regularly remove plants, create re-establishment patches for new plants and provide the right soil, it is all but impossible to produce the same pattern in the garden twice. Weather conditions, seed dispersal, soil-dwelling animal activity, plant competition and gradual humus accumulation can only be controlled to a certain degree. But it is just these aspects that make this kind of gardening exciting. Its allure is captured in the Bed of Inspiration at Fine Molz and Till Hofmann's nursery below.

In 2001, when Fine Molz and Till Hoffman planted a 50 m² (538 sq ft) display bed at their nursery Die Staudengaertnerei in Wald-Michelbach in Germany, they favoured the perennial mixture "Silbersommer" (Silver Summer). They started with a 5 cm (2 in) layer of granite mulch (2–8 mm) to minimize weed growth. They planted according to companionability and because they were looking for a dynamic garden, plants were allowed to self-seed in the years that followed.

By 2004, individual *Stachys byzantina* (lamb's ear) and *Euphorbia cyparissias* (cyprus spurge) had grown into groups, while *Aster sedifolius* (Michaelmas daisy), *Artemisia schmidtiana* 'Nana' (dwarf Schmidt wormwood) and *Anaphalis triplinervis* (triple-nerved pearly everlasting) had become impressive bushes. In gaps that were still open, *Salvia sclarea* (clary sage) and *Verbascum bombyciferum* (mullein) could seed, the former in abundance.

In the following years, the proportion of gaps, and consequently the proportion of clary sage, dwindled. *Knautia macedonica* (Macedonian scabious) became increasingly dominant, as can be seen in this photograph from 2011. Just before the scabious stops flowering, half of them are removed and the rest cut back. *Allium sphaerocephalon* (round-headed leek), *Campanula persicifolia* (bellflower) and *Melica transsilvanica* (red spire) are among the plants that have drifted in and been able to establish themselves.

Allium carinatum subsp. *pulchellum* (keeled garlic) was originally planted in small amounts, but its stand grows ever larger. When the *Knautia* blooming period is over, the keeled garlic provides height again in late summer. Annual mulching with crushed rock (2–3 cm/1–1.5 in) undoubtedly encouraged its spread. After twelve years, individual plant contours are no longer discernible. Some plants have come to dominate while others have (nearly) disappeared, but the minimal maintenance and numerous peaks of flowering have stayed the same.

Waltham Place – naturalism in a formal setting

opposite:
At the edge of the Square Garden, a 2000 m² (½ acre) walled part of the garden, self-seeding plants such as *Verbascum bombyciferum* (mullein), *Centranthus ruber* (red valerian), *Peucedanum verticillare* (giant hog fennel) and *Hieracium maculatum* (spotted hawkweed) grow.

left:
Umbellifers such as *Peucedanum verticillare* (giant hog fennel, surrounded by feather grass), were favourite plants of the late Henk Gerritsen.

Waltham Place, home of the Oppenheimer family since the 1920s, has been transformed into a biodynamic country estate by current owners Nicky and Strilli Oppenheimer. Because the Oppenheimers' sustainable, holistic approach does not conform with traditional landscape design, the historical outer gardens were updated with a more contemporary look.

In 1999, dedicated gardener Strilli Oppenheimer met the Dutchman Henk Gerritsen (1948–2008), who is today considered to be one of the prime influencers in the Dutch Wave movement. His ideas for designing nearly natural plantings that fit within the historical context of the estate gave the gardens of Waltham Place new life. To accord with his credo of working with nature, self-seeding plants play a special role and their contrast with the existing infrastructure of walls, hedges, groves and paths is what brings the whole garden to life. An engaged, creative, conscientious gardening team under the leadership of Beatrice Krehl sees to it that Gerritsen's vision continues to be realized, even after his death.

The Square Garden, which is split down the middle by a pergola, has an interesting history. One of three old kitchen gardens, it was changed to an Italian kitchen garden in 1910 after the purchase of the estate by Carlota Oppenheimer. In 2001, Henk Gerritsen was commissioned to transform it as it was the most distinctive part of the garden. He divided it into three longitudinal parts: the perennial jungle (including *Aconogonon speciosum* 'Johanniswolke', *Gillenia trifoliata* and *Euphorbia cornigera*, among others) and a middle area with lawn, boxwood hedge, path and pond as well as gravel beds with numerous self-seeding plants. The pergola with a rambler rose climbing all over it has remained, under which a central fountain can be found.

A formal pond was merged into the contemporary plan by means of a natural border planting. The space around the sundial is populated by *Hypericum olympicum* (Mount Olympus St John's wort), *Origanum* (oregano) and *Briza maxima* (greater quaking grass).

The northern area was covered with 10 cm (4 in) of gravel in 2001. In winter, this area is completely cleared of plants that have died back. Along with permanent residents such as *Acanthus spinosus* (bear's breeches), shorter-lived plants including *Helleborus argutifolius* (holly-leaved hellebore), *Centranthus ruber* (red valerian) and *Peucedanum verticillare* (giant hog fennel) also influence the character of the garden. *Nassella tenuissima* (feather grass) was also seeded in gravel patches and, after 13 years, has wandered out to the paved paths.

It's hard to imagine how contrasts
could be better orchestrated than this.
In the western Square Garden, the
clear contours of the boxwood hedge
and light green lawn meet in a fog
of *Nassella tenuissima*, out of which
the flowers of *Peucedanum verticillare*
(giant hog fennel) rise. Because of
limited resources between the paving
slabs, giant hog fennel grows only
half as large as it would in a gravel
garden. To the right of the photo,
Genista aetnensis (Mount Etna broom)
reaches gracefully over the lawn and
strengthens the airy atmosphere of this
side of the garden.

The Potager is a former vegetable garden that today is used for cut flowers. Self-seeding plants, along with vegetable plants that are grown for their flowers, play an important role here. To create such a garden requires a lot of knowledge and many interventions. One gardener has the full-time job of cultivating a 1000 m² (¼ acre) plot – self-seeding gardening at its most intense.

Behind the boxwood hedge (from front to back) are lupins, *Silene coronaria* 'Alba' (rose campion), *Centranthus ruber* (red valerian) and *Pastinaca sativa* (parsnip). In the background of the border can be seen violet-blue *Delphinium × elatum* (larkspur) and *Angelica archangelica* (angelica).

Green manure crops are often sown in the kitchen garden, such as *Phacelia tanacetifolia* (fiddleneck) seen here. Self-seeding *Papaver rhoeas* and *P. somniferum* (poppy) are tolerated, as are a few flowering leeks.

In the Potager, decorative and crop plants unite (clockwise from top): *Rumex acetosa* (common sorrel), *Tragopogon porrifolius* (salsify), *Alchemilla mollis* (lady's mantle), *Hemerocallis* (daylily), *Euphorbia griffithii* (spurge), an unknown *Paeonia* species (peony) and *Pastinaca sativa* (parsnip). The sword-shaped leaves in the middle of the picture are from *Crocosmia* 'Lucifer' (montbretia).

121

The 70 m (230 ft) long border once laid out in Gertrude Jekyll style has been allowed to renew itself naturally. *Conium maculatum* (poison hemlock, left), a biennial umbellifer, is thriving. Other self-seeding plants, such as *Aquilegia vulgaris* (columbine), *Silene coronaria* 'Alba' (rose campion), *Anemanthele lessoniana* (New Zealand wind grass) and *Alchemilla epipsila* (lady's mantle) have also found a home here. Permanent residents include *Thalictrum* 'Elin' (meadow rue), *Aruncus* 'Horatio' (goatsbeard), *Euphorbia palustris* (marsh spurge), and behind it *Sambucus* 'Black Beauty'.

The Friar's Walk, just 6 m (20 ft) wide but almost 50 m (165 ft) long, is protected by a high wall so that tender woody plants such as *Magnolia grandiflora* (bull bay), *Punica granatum* (pomegranate) and *Cordyline australis* (cabbage palm) can thrive. Gerritsen foresaw a lush wild perennial underplanting, where he valued the interplay of diverse leaf colours and shapes. An especially successful combination is one of *Inula magnifica* and *Foeniculum vulgare* 'Atropurpureum' (bronze fennel), with an undergrowth of *Origanum laevigatum* 'Hopley' (oregano) and (*Artemisia ludoviciana* var. *latiloba* (wormwood). The expanse is protected by *Magnolia × soulangeana*, while in the background the rose 'Buff Beauty' grows.

The Maze is made by mowing paths in the meadow. To enhance the effect, the expanse is enriched with *Iris sibirica* (Siberian flag). Waltham Place – named England's most beautiful garden in 2011 – is unusual because of its size and its intensive maintenance. However, many of these plantings can be re-created in smaller gardens with much less hired help.

Plants for self-seeding gardens

Nearly every plant that propagates generatively can be used in a self-seeding garden. What follows is a selection of highly recommended species that thrive without problems in most temperate-zone gardens, organized into four categories of use. However, plants do not always fit into only one category, so other potential applications are indicated in each plant's description. Where multiple species are mentioned in a description, the details about the life cycle and recommended methods for establishing are always for the first species named. Since many species have a prolonged period of blooming in summer, this characteristic is not detailed in the descriptions. The plant heights given are for typical gardening conditions; any seed can end up in a less-than-ideal location, so the actual heights of different plants of the same species may vary.

Species for masonry joints, shingle and gravel beds

Plants that fall into this category typically grow deeply penetrating roots that store nutrients and moisture. Once they have germinated and grown sufficiently, these species are able to tolerate a certain amount of stress and surface disturbance.

Unless specified otherwise, all species given here require sunny locations. Species that are especially appropriate for greening garden walls are indicated in their respective descriptions.

Alcea
biennial / seed, plug plant

The single-flowered varieties of *Alcea rosea* (hollyhock) are especially appropriate for gardens of self-seeding plants. This species flowers from early summer to early autumn and is usually biennial.

Hollyhocks prefer deep, fertile, yet not too moist soil. In sites protected from rain, such as close to house walls, they can be short-lived especially when cut back drastically after the last flower withers. Since plants will grow to more than 2 m (6½ ft), they are particularly well suited for positioning at the rear of gardens, but can also make their mark with ground-covering perennials in mixed borders. Flower colour ranges from pink to red to white and the blooming period is early summer.

The Caucasian species *A. ficifolia* is much more robust than *A. rosea* and it can be easily differentiated from other

Alchemilla mollis
long-lived perennial / plug plant

Antirrhinum
short-lived perennial / seed, plug plant

hollyhocks by its large, palmate leaves. Cultivars with the name *A. ficifolia* are usually hybridized with *A. rosea*. These hybrids are susceptible to hollyhock rust, so seek out non-hybrid plants when possible.

Hollyhocks love open sites for optimal development. Crowded plants inhibit one another, causing them to lose their typical character, so make sure that individual plants have sufficient space to develop.

The well-known lady's mantle is an exceptionally hardy, long-lived perennial that has long been used in gardens and public parks. It is not only drought-resistant, but also a strong competitor and highly resistant to pests and diseases; it is not particular about soil quality. Its sulphur-yellow flowers appear from mid to late summer in delicate clusters.

Growing about 30 cm (12 in) tall, lady's mantle is easy to establish in sunny, meadow-like plantings as well as in partial shade. It is an eager self-seeder and seedlings are soon found all around, even in masonry joints and thickets between other plants. Even though this plant will never become a nuisance, it still makes sense to completely prune lady's mantle back after it flowers as this stimulates the production of leaves, giving it a fresh appearance for the second half of the year.

Antirrhinum majus (snapdragon) is primarily a biennial plant but, like the hollyhock, lives longer on very dry sites. Older varieties, still to be found in some cottage gardens, are best for taking over such areas. Thanks to its variable colour, the gardener can decide which colour he or she prefers and select for it.

The 30 cm (12 in) tall *A. braun-blanquetii* (hardy snapdragon) is good for gravel gardens, blooming from early summer to mid-autumn and seeding well.

Centranthus ruber

long-lived perennial / seed, plug plant

The red valerian originated in the Mediterranean and grows wild at fallow sites and on gravel, so provide similar conditions in the garden – gravel beds along external house walls are ideal.

This approximately 1 m (3¼ ft) tall, continuously flowering plant is most common in its red form, but white- and pink-flowered varieties also exist. When several varieties are planted together, a handsome display of colours (including transitional colours) comes to life over time. Light pruning can extend the early to midsummer blooming period into autumn.

Valerian, like *Knautia macedonica* and *Gaura lindheimeri*, is an indispensable continual bloomer that maintains itself in any planting as long as the soil is light enough.

Crambe maritima

long-lived perennial / plug plant

This wonderfully textured and structured plant with its loose heads of small white flowers and fleshy, grey-frosted leaves, cannot be mistaken for any other plant. Even its growth stage is exciting, when its violet-hued leaves begin to unfurl, and it reaches about 50 cm (20 in) when it flowers from early to midsummer. Its beauty really shines when it is planted in combination with *Helianthemum* (rock rose), *Stipa* (feather grass), *Sedum* species (stonecrops), *Eryngium* species (sea hollies) and especially *Eschscholzia californica* (California poppy). It is very long-lived, enchanting gardeners year after year, and germinates in unexpected places.

Echium vulgare

biennial / seed (cold germinating), plug plant

Viper's bugloss is best suited to the driest sites, gravel surfaces and rock gardens, although it also grows in sandy soils. Gravel patches beside buildings that are often boring and sterile can easily be populated with this colourful plant, which grows up to 70 cm (28 in) tall. It especially shines in prairie-style plantings, where its strikingly beautiful inflorescence from mid to late summer can even exceed the beauty of lavender. Together with *Anthemis tinctoria* (dyer's chamomile), *Stipa* (feather grass) or various *Dianthus*, wonderful combinations are possible. Additionally, *Echium vulgare* is a food plant for many butterfly species.

Cultivated varieties are available that are all more or less perennial. Also worth mentioning is *E. russicum*, which is perennial under the right conditions and has candle-shaped flower heads and reddish flowers that are very attractive to bees.

Erigeron karvinskianus
short-lived perennial / plug plant

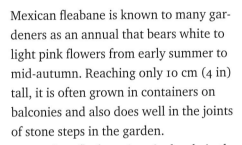

Mexican fleabane is known to many gardeners as an annual that bears white to light pink flowers from early summer to mid-autumn. Reaching only 10 cm (4 in) tall, it is often grown in containers on balconies and also does well in the joints of stone steps in the garden.

Mexican fleabane is quite hardy in the UK, southern Europe and mild southern alpine valleys and has even naturalized in some areas. It also survives the winter at protected sites along the North and Baltic Seas. In northern Germany, plants in masonry joints are hardy but those in borders, though faster growing, die off in winter. Self-seeding plants can only be expected in dry locations with sandy soils.

Eryngium giganteum
biennial or short-lived perennial / seed (cold germinating), initial planting

Giant sea holly comes from the Caucasus and is a biennial or short-lived perennial plant. Once it is established in the garden you can expect to see seedlings popping up for years to come, sometimes in the most unpromising locations. Its alternative common name, Miss Wilmott's ghost, derives from the influential horticulturalist Ellen Willmott (1858–1934), who is said to have surreptitiously spread the seeds of this plant in the gardens of her friends and acquaintances.

Giant sea holly is tolerant of poor soil, though it does well in nutrient-rich, loamy soils with plenty of organic matter. The size of the flowers can vary greatly, as can its height (30–100 cm/12–40 in) and the colour of its silvery upper leaves. The plant is impressive even before its main blooming period from mid to late summer; planted in larger groups, it can seem truly colossal. Considering all its possibilities for using in mixed plantings, it is surprising it is not grown more often.

Propagation is best performed with ripe seed, tapped out of the umbels before winter and directly sown where appropriate. Lightly working seeds into the topsoil or trickling into gravel beds will help with germination. In the first year they produce lime green, ornate leaf rosettes, with flowers appearing in the second year. The multi-branched, silvery seedheads provide winter interest, so cutting back should not be performed until the following spring.

Epilobium dodonaei
short-lived perennial / seed (cold germinating), plug plant

Eschscholzia californica
annual / seed

Euphorbia myrsinites
long-lived perennial / seed (cold germinating), plug plant

The alpine willowherb is relatively short-lived, but it is very attractive and should really be a part of any garden. It bears numerous bright pink flowers and has small, needle-shaped, grey-green leaves held alternately along rather woody stems. The more nutrient-rich the soil, the taller and shorter-lived it becomes; the typical height is around 50 cm (20 in). The flowering period stretches from early to late summer. It likes dry, gravelly soils best, easily populating spaces between other plants. There are also varieties with larger and darker flowers. Alpine willowherb is an important food plant for butterflies and their caterpillars, such as the willowherb hawk moth and the dusky hawk moth.

The California poppy is easy to establish and brings joy to any garden. It has feathery bluish-green leaves and papery flowers that are borne from early summer to early autumn, catching the eye from a distance. There are many varieties in cultivation with creamy-white, orange, yellow or pink flowers. It is at its most magnificent in sandy or gravel soils with full sun. Good drainage is key; in moist soils it is shorter-lived. As a desert dweller that normally would have to complete its life cycle after a short but intense period of rain, it quickly finds appropriate sites in the garden and settles in them.

California poppy maintains itself by dropping its own seed or you can collect the seed and sow it wherever you would like to populate open patches of soil. Spring flowers are quite a bit larger than those that follow in summer and autumn.

The broad-leaved glaucous spurge is an eye-catching, familiar plant that originates from the mountains of southern Europe. A 20 cm (8 in) tall hardy evergreen, it is decorative in gardens even in winter. It needs dry, sandy soil in exposed areas of the garden to be able to propagate by self-seeding. Once established at the right location, *Euphorbia myrsinites* can be enjoyed for many years. It is especially beautiful in combination with *Eschscholzia californica* (California poppy), *Stipa* (feather grass) and other prairie plants.

Because of its diverse origins, its growth habit can vary quite a lot. Not only do the grey leaves vary in size and colour, so too do the flowers, which appear from mid-spring to midsummer, and the seed heads, which range from greenish yellow to golden-yellow.

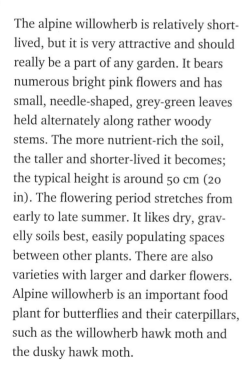

In Rønne, the capital of Bornholm, Denmark, there are numerous stretches of road that are greened with *Alcea rosa* (hollyhock) instead of trees, adding to the charm of the colourful houses. Maintenance of these plants, which bloom for weeks on end, is as minimal as the amount of space they take up.

Gaillardia aristata

short-lived perennial / seed, plug plant

The blanket flower is native to dry grass prairies and rocky steppes in western North America on both sides of the Rockies, but thanks to its liking for the margins of motorways and railways it can now also be found on the Atlantic coast. Because of its origins, *Gaillardia aristata* tolerates dry periods well and even needs them for optimal growth. Lime gravel seems to suit it, but it also grows well in other kinds of rock and gravel where humus is minimal. Under such conditions, *G. aristata* can thrive for several years.

About 40 cm (16 in) tall, it bears its relatively large, luscious yellow flowers with striking reddish disc florets in early and midsummer. The more popular varieties have eye-catchingly colourful, very large individual flowers that are reminiscent of the gerbera daisy, though these produce seed far less frequently than other varieties.

Gaura lindheimeri

short-lived perennial / plug plant

The white gaura comes from Texas, USA, where it grows in sunny open spaces and thin forests. The species principally has white flowers, but there are also cultivated varieties with pink to dark red flowers that are less hardy. Also known as Lindheimer's bee blossom, this plant flowers from late spring until the first frost. Though it is said to be short-lived, this is only the case in soils that are too heavy or too moist; in sandy loam or gravelly soils it lives much longer.

Depending on the variety, the height can vary greatly (50–150 cm/20–40 in). To achieve a more compact growth, cut back plants soon after budding or once the first flower opens. In harsh climates this can be done in early autumn to strengthen shoots for overwintering. Alternatively, you can allow them to develop their own dynamics and give their progeny space to grow in open, light soil.

Helleborus argutifolius

long-lived perennial / plug plant

Despite its Mediterranean origins (Corsica), the holly-leaved hellebore can maintain itself for years in cooler climates given dry, shady, sheltered sites and will even readily self-seed. A handsome plant that produces greenish-yellow flower clusters from early to late spring, it can be grown along a north-east-facing external house wall in a mineral substrate with a gravel mulch. The evergreen, leathery leaves with toothed edges are decorative in their own right.

Stems with withered flowers can be cut back after seeds ripen. Frostbitten stems should be pruned back to the ground in spring. This beautiful shade-loving plant regenerates over summer, developing stems that are 30 cm (12 in) tall. A fully grown plant can easily occupy a square metre (10¾ sq ft).

Hieracium villosum
long-lived perennial / seed (cold germinating), plug plant

The leaves of shaggy hawkweed are equipped with woolly white hairs that help to minimize evaporation, making survival at dry sites possible. Its large yellow flowers appear in midsummer. This tall plant (about 30 cm/12 in) is found in the wild in the limestone Alps and calcareous grasslands of east central Europe and southern Europe. Accordingly, it grows well in gravelly, lime-rich soils, where it readily self-seeds. After flowering, it loses a little of its attractiveness, but be sure to leave at least a few plants for seed when cutting back plants for aesthetic reasons. *H. maculatum* (spotted hawkweed) is a very similar species that stands out with its decoratively marbled leaves. It can produce seed prolifically.

Hordeum jubatum
annual / seed

The name foxtail barley describes the silvery-pink, feathery plumes that are borne from mid to late summer and remain on the plant for a long time, making it prized in the garden. With a height of only 40 cm (16 in), it nevertheless has considerable visual impact as it sways in the breeze. Florists have also slowly come to appreciate foxtail barley's value and it can be seen more and more in long-lasting bouquets.

This plant originates in northern North America and northeast Asia and normally dies off in autumn, but in mild regions it may survive the winter. It can easily grow in various locations in dry borders with light soil and is relatively salt-tolerant. Grow with care, as this plant has the potential to be invasive.

Linaria purpurea
short-lived perennial / seed, plug plant

Purple toadflax comes originally from southern Italy, but it can also be found in the wild in central and western Europe. It is a great companion for roses and tends to bring an airy effect to any planting it is included in, thanks to its delicate form.

This perennial plant prefers fertile soils or light sandy soils. In soils that are too heavy it is fairly short-lived, but maintains itself nonetheless via self-seeding. Its small flowers, which appear between early summer and early autumn, are carried on stems up to 1 m (3¼ ft) tall that are covered in narrow leaves. Colours range between light pink and violet, with occasional white and yellow variations. By collecting seed from plants of various colours, you can ensure colourful progeny that can be managed according to your preference by selective weeding.

With some knowledge of plants and appropriate interventions, you can create species-rich gardens of self-seeding plants. However, it is not essential to use a wide range of plants, since beautiful scenes can easily be created with just a few species. In Bury Court, England, along the edge of a gravel car park that is only occasionally used, *Eschscholzia californica* (California poppy), *Briza maxima* (greater quaking grass) and *Verbascum bombyciferum* (mullein) grow – a combination that looks good for months.

Nassella tenuissima
short-lived perennial / plug plant

Mexican feather grass grows quickly to make a big splash in the garden, but because it is so short-lived it dominates fleetingly. With a height of about 40 cm (16 in) and dense, finely awned seed heads, it resembles an oversized shaving brush.

The seeds of this feather grass are spread all around by the wind. When its seeds ripen, they can easily be harvested by hand and sown the following year for a more targeted seeding. *N. tenuissima* really comes into its own in dry rock gardens and between large stones in the landscape, where large groups of plants make for enchanting scenes in summer and autumn. In mild winters or areas with a climate warm enough for viticulture, plants may survive. In principle, *N. tenuissima* can be paired with any flowering perennial or grass that thrives in similar conditions, for example *Penstemon*.

Oenothera odorata
short-lived perennial / seed, plug plant

This short-lived perennial or often biennial, evening primrose is a magnet for insects. Its fragrant bright yellow flowers start to open in midsummer and continue for several weeks; individual flowers last only one night and wither the following morning, but not before turning a decorative apricot hue. On grey rainy days they may last until noon. The variety 'Sulphurea' grows to about 1 m (3¼ ft) high and has elegant creamy yellow flowers.

Sunny sites in the garden and gravel beds are the preferred locations of this South American species, which comes into its own especially well on path edges and in wide masonry joints. It has no problem maintaining itself through self-seeding, with dispersal of seed often aided by ants, which tend to nest beneath the plant.

Peucedanum verticillare
monocarpic / seed (cold germinating), plug plant

The umbels of giant hog fennel are a perfect substitute for those of the toxic and invasive giant hogweed. It is short-lived, but quickly grows into a handsome solitary plant with burgundy-coloured stems. Its yellow-green umbels bloom in early summer and remain attractive even after they fade.

In addition to fertile, fresh soils, giant hog fennel can also be grown in sandy and gravelly soils. Because of its immense height of more than 3 m (10 ft), choose its location carefully. Selective removal of seedlings is an easy way to keep these plants in the background, where they make an impressive sight. A single plant in a large paving stone joint can be surprisingly effective too.

Salvia sclarea
biennial / seed, plug plant

Several varieties of clary sage exist in the wild, all of which have eye-catching flower heads. The upper leaves may be particularly large and whitish, as with *Salvia sclarea* var. *turkestanica* and varieties from Piedmont, Italy, which have spectacular wine-red flowers. To maintain true-to-type plants, grow either only one variety or plant different varieties far enough apart in the garden to prevent them crossing.

Clary sage is biennial and forms a large, grey-green leaf rosette in the first year. In the second year, from early to late summer, its magnificent flower heads are borne on stems 40–100 cm (16–40 in) tall. The entire plant has a strongly aromatic scent when bruised. It can be grown not only in dry sites such as gravel and prairie gardens, but also in average perennial borders – seedlings often appear in the most unlikely of places, such as in the middle of rose bushes. It is a typical fallow-ground pioneer that does not compete well and quickly disappears when other plants populate the same patch.

Seseli gummiferum
biennial or short-lived perennial / seed (cold germinating), plug plant

This biennial or short-lived perennial with the common name of moon carrot is typical of the umbellifer family (Apiaceae). It requires a location that is sunny, dry and gravelly; the more sun it gets, the more stout and compact its growth. In the first year it produces deeply dissected, silvery-grey leaf rosettes. In the following year, white flower umbels with a pink tinge appear in late summer, the plant reaching about 80 cm (32 in) in height. Among the prettiest companions are grasses, *Antirrhinum* (snapdragon) and *Penstemon*.

Verbena bonariensis

short-lived perennial / seed, plug plant

Argentinian vervain blooms from mid-summer to mid-autumn with purple-violet flower heads. Its hairy, rigid, loosely branched stalks grow to 90–170 cm (3–5½ ft) tall, yet work well in just about any planting. Though it is perennial, it only survives very mild winters. For this reason, it is fairly standard to leave all plants, even those destroyed by frost, in the garden through the winter. In this way plenty of seed is dropped that will germinate for several years. Once integrated into a planting, it is usually able to maintain itself. Seedlings are easily removed or transplanted.

Verbena bonariensis lives longer and seeds better in gravelly soil than in normal garden soil. Its full splendour only unfolds, however, when its relatively high requirements for nutrients and water are met. Even though new plants do not begin to emerge until early summer, they quickly and easily grow taller than their neighbours to establish themselves. Thanks to its attractive purple flowers and elegant growth habit, it can be tempting to populate every corner of the garden with it. Try to avoid the temptation, though, as an overabundance of its buoyant mass of flowers can wreck the structure and beauty of an entire planting.

In ruderal sites, Argentinian vervain can become a garden escape. Exercise caution, especially when the perfect habitat surrounds your garden.

Additional species

Allium carinatum subsp. *pulchellum* (keeled garlic)
Briza maxima (greater quaking grass)
Muscari latifolium (broad-leaved grape hyacinth)
Glaucium flavum (yellow hornpoppy)
Isatis tinctoria (woad)

Allium schoenoprasum
long-lived perennial / seed, plug plant

Few gardeners realize the diversity of sites that chives can thrive in: among rocks in the landscape, in gravel gardens, and also in flower beds. Recently a few strains have appeared that have more intensely coloured flowers and proportionately larger leaf tubes and flower heads than standard varieties. Varieties such as 'Forescate' are used for garden borders, whereas the profusely flowering 'Corsican White' is for gravel gardens. Chives self-seed well and genetic variation provides for a good range of flower colours. The blooming period is from late spring to early summer, with plant heights ranging from 20 to 50 cm (8 to 20 in) depending on the variety. Remove surplus seedlings and individual plants with undesirable flower colours as necessary.

Species for flower borders

Some of the plants in this section are known to us from cottage gardens. To get the best out of them, the soil must be open and regularly cultivated. The plants will reward your efforts, growing fast and flowering prolifically. The long-lived among them will appreciate being protected from competition by conscientious weeding. Fertilization brings positive results in both growth and flower production, but does not extend the lives of the plants. Unless otherwise indicated, full sun is preferred.

Allium aflatunense

long-lived perennial / plug plant

The best-known variety of this 80 cm (32 in) tall flowering onion is the intensely coloured 'Purple Sensation' which spreads quickly, like the species, in suitable sites. The offspring of 'Purple Sensation' grow flower heads of similar sizes to their parents', but the colour varies between dark purple and bright violet. Allowing all the seedlings to grow is usually not an option as they are produced too densely and in great numbers. It is better to thin them to give the remaining plants a chance to grow and flower. *Allium aflatunense* is a heavy feeder that dies relatively quickly from nutrient deficiency, so provide fertilizer and compost.

Many gardeners dislike the tendency of the leaves to wither during flowering, which is typical of this species. This is, however, completely natural and happens with many other species as well. Ideally, surround flowering onion with plants that veil this effect. It flowers from late spring to early summer.

Aquilegia vulgaris

biennial or short-lived perennial / seed (cold germinating), plug plant

Columbines have a romantic quality that ensures these flowering perennials look at home almost anywhere in the garden. The best are the *Aquilegia vulgaris* varieties. Depending on species and variety, columbines can grow to 50–90 cm (20–35 in) tall and require fairly good soil with partial shade, where they flower from late spring to early summer.

Allow selected plants of different colours to bloom and self-seed. Seedlings can be transplanted to free patches in the garden. The following year, allow the new colour mixture to stay or remove any plants of undesirable colours. By strategically removing seedlings, you can achieve a balance that becomes a feast for the eyes when flowering time comes. Maintenance is minimal when using only one variety or strain.

Atriplex hortensis var. rubra
biennial / seed

Red mountain spinach is a cherished cottage garden plant whose green-leaved form has been found in cultivation since time immemorial. The red-leaved, 1 m (3¼ ft) form can achieve beautiful effects, especially in spring when its fresh foliage unfurls itself. Even the progeny of annual red mountain spinach is easy to guide by thinning, transplanting or leaving seedlings. The plant is a long-term provider of colour and creates depth in beds with good soil, though its flowers, lasting from midsummer to early autumn, are very small.

Campanula persicifolia
short-lived perennial / seed, plug plant

This classic wild perennial known as bellflower prefers the partial shade of forest edges, but can grow in a wide range of conditions and peps up any bed of ornamental perennials. In addition to the wild species, which is seldom seen in cultivation, there are large-flowered colourfast strains that breed true to type.

For our purposes here, only the single-flowering types are worth considering, as the double-flowered types tend not to come true from seed and, besides, are not hardy enough. Flower colours range from pure white to light and dark blue. The height range is 50–90 cm (20–35 in) and flowering occurs from early to late summer.

Digitalis
biennial / seed, plug plant

Foxglove grows in the wild on fallow lands and in woodland clearances. In the garden, it works well for a fast and effective planting. The red form in particular is visible from quite a distance.

Digitalis purpurea seeds readily and can become an annoyance if flower heads are not cut back to just a few seed capsules in time. Seedlings are easily removed or transplanted, ideally on a dull day or in light rain. Be sure to observe minimum plant spacing as the leaf rosettes are substantial in size. Thin plants when they are too dense. Foxglove grows to about 1.2 m (4 ft) in height and flowers from early to late summer.

The European native, large yellow foxglove (*D. grandiflora*) thrives in loose, humus-rich and often gravelly soils. At the right site it is very hardy and forms dense clumps on embankments.

Chives are familiar as a kitchen herb, but few realize what a beautiful flowering plant it is when not harvested for the kitchen. Fewer still know that it self-seeds and in time forms large clumps.

Dipsacus fullonum
biennial / seed, plug plant

Common or fuller's teasel, native to Europe, is a very striking biennial ruderal plant that reaches up to 1.5 m (5 ft), is ornamental in character and grows along embankments and scrubland. It requires nutrient-rich soils and does well when introduced into the garden with some plug plants. However, if its site is not rejuvenated by disturbance, this attractive, thistle-like plant will disappear.

Common teasel is not unknown in mixed borders. Its purple flowers in midsummer are pretty, while its dried seed heads remain for a long period of time and its prickly basal leaves have ornamental qualities too. Teasel flowers are rather reminiscent of sea holly (*Eryngium*), but the plant belongs to a different family (Dipsacaceae).

Euphorbia epithymoides
short-lived perennial / seed, plug plant

The many-coloured spurge, or cushion spurge, also known as *Euphorbia polychroma*, is one of the most beautiful spring-flowering plants. It develops a rounded shape about 40 cm (16 in) tall and its flowers appear from mid to late spring; light yellow to golden yellow, held in branched flower heads, they are eye-catching from a distance.

Its location should be as dry as possible, with full sun or partial shade. In heavy, moist soils it will tend to die off and not self-seed well, whereas in gravel gardens or sandy soils it can get out of hand.

A further, underappreciated virtue is its wonderful yellow to bronze colour in autumn. It is a must for every garden and comes into its own in combination with wild tulips, thanks to its early blooming period.

Foeniculum vulgare 'Purpureum'
short-lived perennial / seed, plug plant

Bronze fennel is one of the best-loved and best-known umbellifers of the garden, with dark brown to ochre-coloured leaves that bring diversity to any planting. It can grow up to 1.4 m (4½ ft) tall and flowers from early to late summer. Fennel has no problem producing and dropping seed, though green plants are often to be found among the red-leaved seedlings. These can either be left or weeded out for uniformity. The light yellow, branched umbels of fennel are especially impressive at the start of flowering in early summer, but are also beautiful after flowering and well into winter.

Knautia macedonica
short-lived perennial / seed (cold germinating), initial planting

The wild form of this European native comes from the Balkans and it is now hard to imagine a perennial planting without it. The attractive, ruby-coloured flowers appear primarily from early to late summer on stems up to 1.2 m (4 ft).

The Macedonian scabious needs nutrient-rich soil with good drainage and is tolerant of summer drought. It brings vibrant colour to any sunny border, giving an airy effect. It has the ability to drop sufficient seed to maintain itself, yet does not become invasive. After self-seeding, seedlings are often too dense, but they can either be left to their own devices for the best competitors to emerge or thinned and transplanted elsewhere. Transplant on an overcast day, several at a time. Occasionally, plants with grey-blue, bright pink and bright blue flowers pop up among the otherwise ruby-flowered planting. Remove these to prevent a mixture developing.

Monarda fistulosa subsp. menthifolia
long-lived perennial / plug plant

Wild bergamot or bee balm has several good features: it grows to around 60 cm (2 ft) in height, is completely resistant to mildew and an incredible pizza spice can be made from its flowers. Additionally, this North American species is long-lived and will probably never need to be replanted. It flowers from mid to late summer and consistently self-seeds, crossing occasionally with other bee balm varieties. These hybrids are hardier and healthier than many of the conventional varieties.

If you find the plants unattractive after flowering you can cut them back by about half, which stimulates a small amount of new leaf growth, helping them blend back in with their surroundings. In light soils, remove older plants to benefit younger, more vital ones.

Myosotis sylvatica
biennial / seed

Wood forget-me-nots are invaluable spring-flowering plants. They associate well with with other flowers and produce a traditionally romantic effect with their unmistakable small blue blooms.

This species is usually grown as a biennial and reaches about 40 cm (16 in) tall. Broadcast seed on open soil between other plants and in the foreground of partially shaded beds. Ideally, sow immediately after seed ripens, or failing that in early autumn. Forget-me-nots normally have no problem germinating in humus-rich soil and overwinter in the form of a green leaf rosette. Flowers then appear the following year from mid-spring to midsummer. After flowering, the plants are generally unattractive and can be removed. Collect seeds that have fallen at this time and store them in paper packets.

Nigella damascena
annual / seed

Love-in-a-mist is a popular annual plant whose many-sepalled flowers are on display all summer long and can be preserved for indoor floral displays. Originally from the Mediterranean, it is now cultivated in gardens throughout the world. There are colourful dwarf varieties that grow to only 20 cm (8 in) high as well as taller strains and colour mixtures.

Once established, love-in-a-mist maintains itself by dropping seed and seedlings can easily be thinned or transplanted. As young plants die off in wet or very cold winters, sow in spring where winters are harsh. It partners well with *Eschscholzia* and *Gaura lindheimeri* in dry, sunny sites with sandy soil.

Onopordum acanthium
biennial / seed, plug plant

The cotton thistle is a spectacular solitary plant that is found from Europe to central Asia on fertile, rocky slopes and margins. A biennial, it easily establishes in dry parts of the garden with a few seeds. Enormous, silvery-grey leaf rosettes form in the first year, which are impressive in themselves. The plants require quite a bit of space as they can reach up to 1 m (3¼ ft) in diameter and may inhibit other plants. Flowers come the following year, when the plant can grow to up to 3 m (10 ft) tall.

Cotton thistle is ideal for the background of a dry bed; planting along the path invites injury from its sharp thorns. The violet-red flowers, which appear from midsummer to early autumn, contrast impressively with the silvery-grey vegetation. Removing most seed heads before they drop helps to prevent over-seeding the garden. The trick is to keep just a few plants at the desired location.

In some parts of the garden, let things grow wild. This scene with *Digitalis purpurea* (foxglove), *Papaver somniferum* (opium poppy) and *Nigella damascena* (love-in-a-mist) is made possible by regular cultivation of the seedbeds. (De Sequoiahof, Netherlands).

Orlaya grandiflora
annual / seed

The white laceflower is a stunning plant with umbels of wide petals that are marvellous adornments during its blooming period of early to late summer. Its relatively large, hairy fruits are also unmistakable. Seed can be hard to come by, but if you are able to get your hands on some, you should definitely give this tall (40 cm/16 in) plant a try. It prefers sunny and dry patches with fertile soil and grows in meadows and forest edges. It self-seeds without becoming a nuisance.

Papaver
annual / seed

In country gardens, *Papaver somniferum* (opium poppy) is just the right plant, as it provides traditional colours and flower shapes. By picking the seed capsule and shaking it over the soil, you can spread seed where you would like poppies to grow; they will overwinter in the upper layer of the topsoil and germinate the following year. In this way, you can sow just those seeds of the varieties you desire at exactly the right location. The dark plum-coloured varieties are highly sought after, and these can be selected out and sown in time to flower from mid to late summer. The grey-green, wide leaf of the opium poppy is conspicuous and typical of the genus. The plant grows to about 80 cm (32 in) in height.

Cultivated varieties of opium poppy are heavier feeders than wild poppies, which do fine on meagre soils. No license or permit is required to grow opium poppy in the UK.

P. orientale (Oriental poppy), which comes from Iran, produces less seed than opium poppy. Orange, red and white varieties are in cultivation. It is important that they get plenty of light in autumn, as leaves sprout and grow in late summer and then overwinter. In late spring and summer, they like it dry.

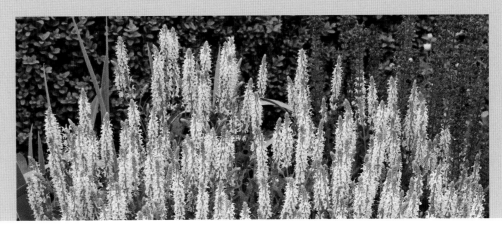

Rudbeckia triloba
biennial or short-lived perennial / seed (cold germinating), plug plant

Brown-eyed susan is a popular species and justifiably so. Unlike other coneflowers, it is long-lasting as a cut flower and can be used in bouquets. Its yellow-gold flowers are relatively small (4 cm/1½in), but they come in great numbers on branched stalks. Its growth habit can make it seem massive within a given planting as it blooms from late summer to mid-autumn. Especially when standing alone, it can reach a height of 1.4 m (4½ ft).

Rudbeckia triloba seeds lightly in loose, sandy-loam soils. It fills every space with seedlings, which are quickly and easily removed if required. In autumn, be sure to leave some seed heads to ensure the coming of the next generation.

Salvia nemorosa
short-lived perennial / seed, plug plant

Balkan clary comes with a long list of cultivated varieties that differ in height (30–70 cm/12–28 in) and flower colour (blue, violet or white). You will have to try a particular variety to find out how well it self-seeds. Several varieties are sterile, coming from hybrids, but many plants are available commercially from open-pollinated seed that are more appropriate for our purposes here – though purer strains are often less attractive, with duller colours. Some vegetatively propagated varieties give rise to a wider range of colour in the flowers of their offspring – even pink or red flowers are possible. Cutting back after the first flowering in early summer will produce a second flowering in late summer or early autumn that typically lasts until the frosts. If Balkan clary is to maintain itself by seed be sure to allow at least some plants to produce seed. As it originates in the steppes of Hungary and the drylands of the Balkans, *Salvia nemorosa* appreciates well-drained, light garden soils and full sun.

There are also other sage species with similar needs that are cultivated, including *S. argentea*, *S. aethiopis*, *S. amplexicaulis* and *S. nutans*.

Silene coronaria
biennial / seed, plug plant

The rose campion is an imposing presence in the garden during its blooming period from mid to late summer. Its striking, felty, grey leaf rosette suggests a plant that likes light, dry, mineral-rich soils, but in fact the best specimens are found in normal, healthy garden soils in full sun.

Brilliant purple-red flowers, whose colour is so vibrant it can be difficult to place them well with other plants, are held on long, branched stalks. Some varieties with subtler colours may be easier to match with plants in the garden, such as the pure white 'Alba' or the less familiar 'Oculata' (also known as 'Angel Blush'), which is white with a pink "eye".

Rose campion readily self-seeds and grows to about 80 cm (32 in) in height. Seedlings appearing in the wrong space are easily transplanted.

Silene viscaria
long-lived perennial / seed, plug plant

In the wild, the sticky catchfly is found primarily in dry, calcareous grasslands, where plants have plenty of room to spread out. As a garden plant, it therefore prefers a similar situation, even though it tolerates different locations well and is effective as a gap-filler in flower beds. Sticky catchfly grows to 20–50 cm (8–20 in) tall, flowers from late spring to early summer and is available in numerous cultivated varieties.

Tragopogon porrifolius
biennial / seed, plug plant

The violet flowers of salsify appear in early to midsummer. Even more decorative than the flowers are the dandelion-like, round seed heads, which can be up to 15 cm (6 in) in diameter. Unfortunately, the pappus-crowned seeds do not stay on the plant for long, falling in every possible direction from the plant soon after ripening. For this and several other related species originating in southern Europe, self-seeding is the standard method of propagation; they maintain themselves in the garden when the surroundings and soil conditions are what they require.

Salsify is a ruderal plant that also maintains itself well in dry grasslands. It is usually biennial with a height of 50–80 cm (20–32 in).

Verbascum

biennial / seed, plug plant

Mullein, which flowers from early spring to early autumn, enriches plantings with its vertical structure. Most of the species are biennial and form a leaf rosette in the first year that requires plenty of space for optimal development. If you find you have too many plants in one border, extra ones can easily be removed. Transplanting is only successful with young plants.

Most *Verbascum* species come from the eastern Mediterranean and Asia Minor, though some can also be found in central Europe on dry slopes. They mostly form felty, grey leaf rosettes, though some species such as *V. phoeniceum* have dark green leaves. The most common species are *V. olympicum*, *V. densiflorum* and *V. bombyciferum*, which live longer when cut back to about 30 cm (12 in) above the ground at the end of the blooming period. To increase the number of plants, seed heads should be left on to allow them to drop seed. Depending on the species, the height ranges from 1 m (3¼ ft) up to 2.5 m (over 8 ft).

Verbena hastata

short-lived perennial / seed (cold germinating), plug plant

Blue vervain is a very hardy, prolifically seeding species from North America. Its long blooming period and undemanding character make it a valuable addition to the garden. The flowers sit in small, pyramidal flower spikes, which in turn are part of a candelabra-like growth habit. *Verbena hastata* grows up to 1.2 m (4 ft) tall and there are blue, pink and white varieties, making for a wonderful array of colours when they are planted together. Even if blue vervain does not stand quite as upright as *V. bonariensis*, at least part of the plant should be allowed to remain through the winter for its pretty shape and profuse progeny the following year. To extend the already long blooming period of midsummer to early autumn or to reduce the size of the plant, cut back several times a year.

Additional species

Agrostemma githago (corn cockle)
Ammi majus (bullwort)
Anethum graveolens (dill)
Angelica archangelica (angelica)
Angelica gigas (purple angelica)
Calendula officinalis (marigold)
Centaurea montana (great blue-bottle)
Coreopsis tinctoria (golden tickseed)
Hibiscus cannabinus (kenaf, ambari hemp)
Lupinus (lupin)
Molopospermum peloponnesiacum (striped hemlock)
Papaver rhoeas (common poppy)
Oenothera glazioviana (red-sepal evening primrose)
Oenothera versicolor (Mexican evening primrose)
Pastinaca sativa (parsnip)
Scabiosa ochroleuca (pale yellow scabious)
Scandix pecten-veneris (shepherd's needle)
Zinnia peruviana (Peruvian zinnia)

Achillea millefolium
short-lived perennial / seed, plug plant

Species for sunny perennial plantings

Plants of this group differ from border plants in that they do not seed so prolifically and do not necessarily require loosening of the soil for them to re-establish themselves. Their survival strategy is to grow in locations where gaps in the vegetation occur. These could be low-nutrient sites, where the soil is never completely covered, or meadows. The more the site in the garden resembles the plant's natural environment, the more you can count on the plant establishing itself. Without light that reaches their seeds, these species cannot grow new plants.

The pure, unhybridized form of yarrow is short-lived and rarely seen in cultivation, but it maintains itself via self-seeding, which is most successful in lighter soils. In some gardens, it is badly damaged by slugs.

By introducing plug plants with diverse flower colours, you can create interesting mixtures of colour in the garden. Older varieties, containing more *Achillea millefolium* "blood", are more likely to maintain themselves with the dual strategy of producing seed and sending out runners than are modern hybrids. One colour can be favoured by removing individuals of other colours. Plants reach a height of about 50 cm (20 in) and bloom from early summer to early autumn.

Allium sphaerocephalon
long-lived perennial / plug plant

Like many other alliums, round-headed garlic self-seeds well, provided the location is right – given a dry, sandy soil it can populate it in large groups. Its dark ruby flowers combine well with its surroundings and it is ornamental even after its summer flowering period. Round-headed garlic grows up to 70 cm (28 in) and is especially handsome when paired with yellow-flowered members of the daisy family (*Asteraceae*). Its leaves are very narrow, meaning it barely impinges upon its neighbours and it is rarely necessary to reduce it.

Althaea cannabina
long-lived perennial / plug plant

Along with *Gaura lindheimeri* and other plants preferring arid climates, the tall (1.5 m/5 ft), long-flowering palm-leaf marshmallow maintains itself for years in the garden by self-seeding. Grasses such as *Stipa calamagrostis* and *Calamagrostis brachytricha* accentuate its delicate vegetation and compliment it superbly. Its dark pink-coloured flowers first appear in early summer and last almost until autumn.

Althaea cannabina has the ability to take over an entire bed in a matter of years but can be limited to a few large groups of plants. Do not cut back until spring so that it can drop seed over the winter that then germinates over the course of the spring. Only young seedlings can be transplanted with ease.

Anthemis tinctoria
short-lived perennial / seed, plug plant

Dyer's chamomile makes a valuable contribution to a planting of self-seeding species, not least because it reproduces best in very poor soils. Some varieties are fairly short-lived and should be treated as annuals. A yellow variety from Turkey named 'Ala Dagh', which grows to a height of about 40 cm (16 in), makes for a great initial planting. It has tiny composite flowers that appear in early summer and can be maintained until early autumn by pruning. Most other varieties have larger flowers in pretty pastel colours, but the only way to make them live longer is to rigorously cut them back nearly to the ground and they rarely self-seed. The best of these other varieties is probably Piet Oudolf's 'Sauce Hollandaise', which overwinters well without cutting back.

Anthericum ramosum
long-lived perennial / plug plant

The spider plant spreads well via self-seeding, provided the soil is rocky, light, drains well and is high in lime. This charming, white-flowered perennial also does well in heavier soils, but will not usually self-seed. There is a wide range in plant height according to variety, from 40 cm (16 in) to 1.2 m (4 ft). The blooming period is from mid to late summer.

Colourful, apparently natural groupings can be planted by combining *Anthemis tinctoria* (dyer's camomile), *Echium vulgare* (viper's bugloss), *Dianthus cruentus* (blood pink), *Verbascum* (mullein), *Linum perenne* and *L. austriacum* (flax), *Stipa* (feather grass) and *Geranium sanguinemum* (bloody cranesbill). Depending on the nature of the soil, one of the other species may come to dominate over time.

Artemisia absinthium
short-lived perennial / plug plant

You can create truly beautiful beds with wormwood if you keep control of it; in light soils in hot, dry climates, it is in its element to such a degree that it constantly spreads by seed. Its silvery foliage can be highly decorative, giving a sense of extravagance to any bed. Once you have established a mature plant at the right location, timely pruning prevents further spreading by seed if this is what you wish. This 50 cm (20 in) high plant becomes woody at its base, making it appear more bushy. Combinations with annual flowers and wide-leaved perennials make for beautiful scenes that last for weeks or even months. Its attraction is the foliage, the midsummer flowers being fairly insignificant. Wormwood likes full sun and is good for gravel beds.

Anthriscus sylvestris 'Ravenswing'
short-lived perennial / seed (cold germinating), plug plant

Although common cow parsley is not often cultivated, this dark-leaved variety is popular. It is a biennial or short-lived perennial plant that grows to about 80 cm (32 in) in height. In the first year it develops a dark brown, almost black rosette, then from the second year it blooms with small-branched white umbels in late spring and early summer. Self-seeding can be virtually guaranteed, but you can expect to find green-leaved plants that will need to be culled. Cow parsley can be used to make the most stunning displays, as long as the soil is not too dry or nutrient-rich. It is especially handsome in combination with large-flowered perennials and adds charm to a natural garden.

Plants with brownish flowers are rarely seen as gardenworthy, but it pays to look at the plant as a whole and in the context of its surroundings. *Bupleurum longifolium* (hare's ear), here seen as a bronze-flowered variety in the garden at Bury Court in the UK, works splendidly with its broad light green foliage set against slender grasses.

Bupleurum longifolium
short-lived perennial / plug plant

This species of hare's ear should be used more than it is, as its long blooming period stretches from late spring to early autumn and makes it a distinctive companion with its tiny yellow flowers surrounded by copper-coloured bracts. Limy, rocky soils help this 70 cm (28 in) high plant to self-seed more effectively. Fully grown plants have a bushy, spreading habit which makes them decorative throughout the entire growing season, especially when teamed with *Geranium sanguineum* (bloody cranesbill), *Stipa* (feather grass), *Artemisia* (wormwood) and *Gaura*.

Calamagrostis brachytricha
long-lived perennial / plug plant

Korean feather reed grass, with its unusual panicles, brings considerable presence to the garden. Originating from Korea and Japan, this upright, tufted grass reaches its maximum height of 1.2 m (4 ft) in early to mid-autumn. With its finely branched panicles, which can be up to 40 cm (16 in) long, it is incredibly beautiful, especially when covered in frost and dewdrops. In heavy soils, it is impermanent but in well-drained sites it is very stable.

Korean feather reed grass maintains itself through self-seeding without getting out of hand. Where there are gaps, it fills them readily. It does, however, require sites with full sun that are well-drained. In light, sandy soils it tends to spread so it should be avoided in sensitive areas or only planted where it cannot escape into the wild.

Geranium pratense
long-lived perennial / plug plant

The European meadow cranesbill, true to its name, is best suited to meadow-like plantings but works in borders, too. In the wild, it populates rarely mown slopes and meadows, where fertile, moisture-retentive soils predominate. Full sun is required for the plant to truly thrive. When these conditions are present, it self-seeds readily.

There are many varieties and colours available. The height of the plants is 80 cm (32 in) and colours range from pure white to every shade of blue to violet, with the blooming period stretching from early to late summer. Unfortunately, this plant is usually afflicted with powdery mildew by the end of flowering, though this can be kept under control by cutting it back to ground level. That means having gaps in the borders for a short time, but the plants quickly grow back to make

Leucanthemum vulgare
short-lived perennial / seed, plug plant

Linum
long-lived perennial / seed, plug plant

a handsome scene in late autumn. Be sure to wait until seeds have fallen from this plant before pruning to ensure the next generation.

Geranium pratense hybridizes easily with closely related species such as *G. himalayense* or *G. clarkei* when they grow nearby, creating interesting shapes and colours. All varieties with plenty of *G. pratense* "blood" self-seed well, though seed production can vary. It takes a fair amount of time to establish a population. Another possibility for propagation is via cuttings in spring.

Ox-eye daisy, a European native, is universally loved and it is hard to imagine doing without it in a naturalistic garden. The wild version has small flowers, propagates by self-seeding on ruderal patches and calcareous grasslands and grows to around 70 cm (28 in) tall. Several large-flowered varieties such as 'Rheinblick' have long been in cultivation and are robust and hardy. Before cutting any plants back, make sure there are enough mature plants that will be strengthened and stimulated by the cut back to flower more. Alternatively, a patch can develop its own dynamics when it is largely left alone. Ox-eye daisy flowers from late spring to early summer.

Perennial blue flax (*Linum perenne*) distinguishes itself with its clear blue flowers that open in the morning on sunny days from early to midsummer. It is not only highly variable in habit and flower colour, it can also range from 30 to 60 cm (1 to 2 ft) in height depending on the variety and subspecies. In the wild, it grows in light, dry soils and given these in the garden it will effortlessly self-seed. *L. austriacum* is a very similar species with larger, azure blue flowers. It is seldom seen in cultivation, though it is even more impressive.

Some plants cannot be limited to one spot as proven here by *Leucanthemum vulgare* (ox-eye daisy) in a wall at Great Dixter in England. Once it has settled in a masonry joint, ox-eye daisy puts on a pretty display that lasts all summer long, stealing the show from more traditional wall plants.

Polemonium caeruleum
long-lived perennial / seed, plug plant

In the garden, Jacob's ladder self-seeds reliably in nutrient-rich soils only. This Central European native is found in the wild in meadows and along riverbanks, bearing large bluish-violet (and sometimes white) flowers in loose clusters from early to midsummer. Cultivated varieties can be shorter-lived, but also self-seed when soil conditions are appropriate. Depending on location, it can grow from 40 cm (16 in) to 1 m (3¼ ft) in height.

Rudbeckia fulgida var. deamii
long-lived perennial / plug plant

This prairie plant called Deam's coneflower is not widely known, but it has long been grown in home gardens. Its main advantages are drought resistance and its ability to deal with poorer soils. This variety has been somewhat forgotten because of the popularity of *Rudbeckia fulgida* var. *sullivantii* 'Goldsturm'. Though it produces seed prolifically, it always stays within certain limits and thus never becomes invasive.

As opposed to the much wider-leaved Goldsturm coneflower, *R. fulgida* var. *deamii* has broadly ovate, pointed, hairy leaves; the stalk leaves are sparsely toothed. Its golden-yellow ray petals are shorter and surround brownish-black disc florets. The blooming period is from late summer to early autumn, with the flowers carried on stems 60–90 cm (2–3 ft) in height.

R. laciniata is another coneflower with bright yellow flowers that bloom from midsummer to early autumn, though it is rarely grown. It can quickly take over beds via runners, yet does not become a nuisance. The height range is 1.2–2 m (4–6½ ft). Another appropriate species is *R. subtomentosa* from the American Midwest, which has small but numerous flowers.

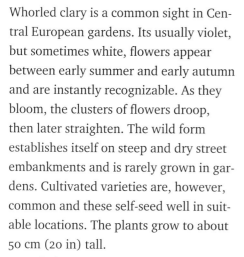

Salvia verticillata
long-lived perennial / seed, plug plant

Whorled clary is a common sight in Central European gardens. Its usually violet, but sometimes white, flowers appear between early summer and early autumn and are instantly recognizable. As they bloom, the clusters of flowers droop, then later straighten. The wild form establishes itself on steep and dry street embankments and is rarely grown in gardens. Cultivated varieties are, however, common and these self-seed well in suitable locations. The plants grow to about 50 cm (20 in) tall.

In light soils and in gravel gardens, whorled clary self-seeds so well as to get out of hand, though seedlings can be quickly and easily removed. It does well in heavy soils, too, where it also self-seeds. Its seedlings can be transplanted easily once they have reached a certain size.

Sanguisorba
long-lived perennial / plug plant

The *Sanguisorba* genus (burnet) offers flowers in a wide array of colours and sizes that bloom at various periods from early summer to mid-autumn. They may be upright or pendant. Nearly all species of burnet demand loamy, fairly moist soil; when the location is too dry, some are susceptible to mildew. Most species develop a thick, woody root within a few years, making it difficult to move the plant. First-year plants, on the other hand, are fairly easy to transplant.

In meadow gardens as well as in moist, partially shaded forest edges, burnet self-seeds without problem and hybridizes readily. *Sanguisorba officinalis* varieties such as the short, dark red 'Tanna' (60 cm/2 ft) and the tall 'Pink Elephant' (1.5 m/5 ft) are particularly likely to hybridize, especially when strains of *S. tenuifolia* var. *alba* (1.7 m/5½ ft), with its pendant white flowers, are in the vicinity. This can lead to flowers with wonderful shapes and colours. The species *S. hakusanensis* (60 cm/2 ft) and *S. obtusa* (1 m/3¼ ft) also cross-pollinate when the environment is right and create an opulent display.

Valeriana officinalis
long-lived perennial / seed, plug plant

Garden valerian, once planted, can maintain itself in nearly any soil. A single plant that produces plenty of seed is sufficient to ensure the next generation. Valerian can be anywhere from 30 cm (12 in) to 1.5 m (5 ft) in height. Its pink to white flowers, which appear in high summer, sit on an umbrella-like cyme and have a light aroma. Seedlings must be transplanted before they develop a turnip-like root to have any chance of success.

Loamy, occasionally waterlogged, soil is ideal for valerian. Once plants have established in the desired location, their spread can be discouraged by cutting back before seed has formed and ripened. Established plants are very long-lived and are stable for years. Valerian leaves turn a pretty shade of yellow in autumn but then give off a rather unpleasant odour.

Verbesina alternifolia
long-lived perennial / plug plant

The golden honeyplant is easily recognizable by its asymmetrical yellow flowers, which are borne in a spherical corymb during high summer. Up to 2 m (6½ ft) tall, this prairie plant requires good soil and quickly grows into loose, stable tufts. Impressive stands can be established purely by self-seeding, which can be particularly dramatic in front of a dark wooded background. The golden honeyplant does well in full sun or light shade.

Additional species

Echinops sphaerocephalus (globe thistle)
Heliopsis helianthoides var. *scabra* (North American ox-eye)
Molinia arundinacea (purple moor-grass)
Papaver atlanticum (atlas poppy)
Patrinia scabiosifolia (eastern valerian)
Penstemon digitalis 'Husker Red' (penstemon)
Primula veris subsp. *veris* (cowslip)
Symphyandra pendula (pendulous bellflower)
Verbascum phoeniceum (purple mullein)

Anemone nemorosa
long-lived perennial / plug plant

Species for partial and full shade

Species that are suitable for partial and full shade spread slowly by self-seeding. A few spring ephemerals attempt to avoid the shade of trees by growing early, before the trees are in leaf, whereas others persevere despite the lack of light. In addition to open soil, minimal root competition and a small amount of light, these plants need sufficient water to be able to establish themselves. It can help to collect fallen leaves, shred them, and spread them as mulch.

The wood anemone self-seeds well under woody plants in mature gardens that have a well-established humus layer. This is especially the case for varieties with single white flowers, which grow 10–20 cm (4–8 in) tall and bloom in mid-spring. Along with other spring ephemerals with underground storage organs such as *Eranthis* (winter aconite) and *Galanthus* (snowdrop), wood anemone slowly forms a colourful blanket that lasts for years. Make sure you have a diverse mixture of plants that are interesting in the summer after wood anemone withers and goes dormant.

Brunnera macrophylla
long-lived perennial / plug plant

Siberian bugloss is able to spread by self-seeding and become established in situations where the soil is not too dry and sufficiently deep. Under flowering cherries, these dense, 40 cm (16 in) high plants with small blue flowers are a feast for the eyes in mid-spring. Later, the large, heart-shaped leaves provide groundcover. Reducing the colony will not be necessary for several years and should be done by digging plants up with a spade, as each root is capable of sending up new shoots.

Siberian bugloss combines best with short-lived perennials such as *Aquilegia* (columbine) or other perennials with similar competitive strategies.

Campanula
short-lived perennial / plug plant

The bellflower species *Campanula trachelium* and *C. rapunculoides* can turn into weeds if you do not check their spread. Nevertheless, they beautify forest edges, gardens and parks. Ideally, plant larger groups that require little care.

The nettle-leaved bellflower (*C. trachelium*) does well in a shaded situation with dry soil, so you could try populating the area under conifers. Improve the soil slightly first, to encourage germination then, after successful propagation, plant out hardened-off young plants. Bellflowers grow to 50–90 cm (20–35 in) and flower throughout the summer.

Cortia wallichiana
long-lived perennial / plug plant

Milk parsley is an exquisite umbellifer that is hardy and long-lived. Its primary blooming period is early to midsummer, but it produces its 10 cm (4 in) diameter umbels of white flowers deep into autumn. It is also very decorative out of the flowering season, standing 1.2 m (4 ft) tall with fresh green, parsley-like foliage.

Ideal locations in the garden are sunny to lightly shaded with good soil that is not too dry. Beautiful garden displays can be composed with this "king of umbellifers". The plant is sometimes still listed under its former botanical name, *Selinum wallichianum*.

Corydalis solida subsp. transsylvanica
long-lived perennial / plug plant

Fumewort, with its eye-catching flowers, creates a palpable air of spring in the garden. As with *Eranthis* (winter aconite) and *Helleborus* (Christmas rose), this effect only comes to life when a sufficient amount of seed is planted.

Most fumeworts come from forests and forest edges and grow well in any humus-rich soil with leaf litter, as long as young plants are not destroyed by constant pedestrian traffic and/or cultivation. When it is time for this hardy spring bloomer to drop seed, the area must be left alone as much as possible. Fumewort seeds are coated with a fleshy structure that is attractive to ants, which carry them away ensuring seed dispersal. Every year more and more seedlings come up, slowly increasing the size of the carpet of pink to red flowers that bloom in early spring. For our purposes, a few individuals of the right colour will suffice. From seed to the first flowering takes about three years, so it will take several years before the patch really comes to life. Plants reach a height of 10–20 cm (4–8 in).

Appropriate spots for planting fumewort are between hellebores and other partial-shade-loving perennials. A light dressing with lime and well-rotted compost helps to speed up propagation.

Crocus tommasinianus
long-lived perennial / plug plant

Crocus tommasinianus is the perfect crocus for self-seeding, though it is only appropriate for large gardens. Just a few starter bulbs are all you need to bring this valuable pre-spring flower into your garden. Early crocus grows to be 10–15 cm (4–6 in) tall, seeds quickly and has its seeds distributed by ants. There are several different-coloured strains available that are all sterile, as long as no other varieties are present, especially of the same species. If so they will cross, producing mixed variations that pale in comparison to their parents. Early crocus works well in meadow-like plantings or between shrubs.

Cyclamen
long-lived perennial / plug plant

As with many other spring bulbs, two hardy cyclamen species are all you need to start with. The best location for them is under hazel shrubs or other deep-rooted woody plants in partial shade. There are extremely beautiful strains of eastern cyclamen (*Cyclamen coum*) with crimson, pink or white flowers. Just a few individuals will in time self-seed and, within a few years, grow into a colourful carpet. The flowers of this 10 cm (4 in) high plant appear in late winter if the season is a mild one.

Another decorative and undemanding species is *C. hederifolium*, which has leaves reminiscent of ivy. Its deep pink to white flowers appear from midsummer to early autumn. Seeds of both species are transported by ants and germinate in surprising locations. The important thing is to leave patches with seedlings alone and not disturb them by cultivation.

Deschampsia cespitosa
long-lived perennial / plug plant

Tufted hair grass is probably the least picky of any hardy plant in terms of situation, readily thriving in shallow water, shade or gravel gardens. This grass works well with woodland and forest edge plantings and puts on an impressive display with its fine, feathery panicles of silvery-purple flowers in summer. If your initial planting comprises only one named variety or one clone, few or no seedlings may come up. When several varieties are planted, ideally flowering at the same time, it may seed prolifically. Depending on variety and type, blooming can occur from midsummer to early autumn. The plant height may be anywhere from 50 cm (20 in) to 1.2 m (4 ft).

Eranthis hyemalis
long-lived perennial / plug plant

Winter aconite gradually carpets the ground to create beautiful displays in late winter and early spring. It is 10–15 cm (4–6 in) tall and needs to be strategically introduced into the garden. Because planting tubers meets with little success and is time-consuming, the recommended method is to transplant individuals from large stands shortly after flowering. Alternatively, you can broadcast seed into a prepared seedbed where you want the plants, but this requires freshly harvested seed that is allowed to complete its ripening in paper packets for 14 days. The seed germinates the following year. It is crucial not to disturb the patch, so weed it by hand rather than hoe.

Euphorbia dulcis 'Chameleon'

long-lived perennial / plug plant

The standard form of sweet spurge elicits little interest from gardeners, but this 40 cm (16 in) high plant from the Dordogne in France is very popular. It has a spectacular dark-red leaf colour, which changes throughout the year and can even be orange-red to copper-coloured. Its blooming period in late spring is relatively uninteresting. The important thing to know is that the colour of the strain comes true from seed. Its natural habitat is a dry forest edge, but it can also be used to fill gaps between tall plants in beds.

Euphorbia lathyris

biennial / seed

Caper bush has long been known to gardeners and is often planted in the hope of driving away moles. Whatever the reason for cultivation, it can maintain itself by prolifically self-seeding. Its regular arrangement of grey-green lance-shaped leaves makes for an interesting sight. The flowers are borne in midsummer, but do not change the appearance of the plant much. Caper bush can grow to be about 1 m (3¼ ft) tall.

Galanthus nivalis

long-lived perennial / plug plant

In larger areas in gardens it is easy to establish impressive expanses of common snowdrop, though you will need plenty of patience. This European native likes light sandy loam soils and partial shade and grows to a height of about 20 cm (8 in). A thin layer of leaf litter on the ground makes for ideal growth because snowdrops are found in damp, low-lying woodlands in the wild and are therefore heavier feeders than you might expect.

Snowdrop bulbs are ideally planted in early autumn so that they can send out roots before winter. Alternatively, you can divide clumps during or immediately after flowering in late winter/early spring and plant them in appropriate locations. It takes three to four years for the first flowers to appear and another four to five years before handsome clumps have formed.

In a mature garden, *Hyacinthoides hispanica* (Spanish bluebell) has slowly spread throughout the years by self-seeding. The combination with other, non-self-seeding plants such as the white-flowering *Smilacina racemosa* (spikenard) creates a wonderful display.

Geranium phaeum

long-lived perennial / plug plant

The dusky cranesbill is a plant that spreads well in the right site, providing diversity of shape and colour and a natural effect. In the wild, the plant is found in damp, low-lying woodlands where it forms stands. Light partial shade is the ideal location and here it can even withstand drought.

There are several varieties, with flower colour from white to pink, red, brown, violet and almost black, that must be vegetatively propagated. Several have highly decorative leaves that are reminiscent of zonal geraniums and are prominent carrying their marbled coloration deep into autumn.

Some varieties of dusky cranesbill grow up to 80 cm (1¾ ft) tall. It has a bad reputation in conventional gardening because it self-seeds, which is undesirable in that context but an advantage for our purposes. It is important to strike a balance between taller and shorter plants and the form that will dominate long-term depends on several environmental factors. To encourage ornamental leaves, try regularly adding varieties such as 'Angelina', 'Saturn' or 'Samobor'.

Wood cranesbill (*Geranium sylvaticum*) is an accommodating alternative that grows in the wild in meadows as well as mountain forests and can therefore tolerate full sun to full shade. Its blooming period is very brief, but is wonderful in light shade. The soil needs to be somewhat moist in spring and the situation needs to be sunny all year round. The wood cranesbill can be an ideal early bloomer in between later-blooming shrubs. Once established, it delights year in and year out and continually surprises with its diversity of colour and shape.

Helleborus foetidus

short-lived perennial / seed, plug plant

The stinking hellebore is one of the most structural plants in the garden during winter and spring and it has a striking leaf texture. Once established, it propagates readily and slowly covers entire expanses underneath and near trees. It requires a loose, nutrient-rich and humus-rich soil. Lime is not absolutely necessary but certainly helps these plants thrive. It does well even in gravel gardens and its blooms are eye-catching during the cold seasons. There are several varieties of diverse origins available, though 'Wester Flisk' with its dark red leaf stems and light yellow upper leaves is probably the best known.

Stinking hellebore is not very long-lived, but maintains itself well through prolific seed production and grows to 40–60 cm (16–24 in) tall. Seeds are distributed beyond the base of the plant by ants. It combines well with *Corydalis solida* subsp. *transsylvanica*, *Anemone nemorosa* and *Ranunculus ficaria* to form colourful garden displays.

Helleborus × hybridus
long-lived perennial / plug plant

Hesperis matronalis
short-lived perennial / seed, plug plant

Hybrid Lenten roses have become popular thanks to modern selections and colourful strains. Until about 20 years ago, they were only to be found in connoisseurs' gardens. The large-flowered, spotted and double-flowered varieties common today were a long time coming, because Lenten roses require three years before the first flowering and several more years before becoming mature plants of about 50 cm (20 in) in height.

Once flowering in early and mid-spring is over, seeds ripen within fruits which burst open to release the seeds over a few days in early summer. Collecting the opened fruits enables you to deliver seed to places where you want your Lenten roses to grow and the faster the *Helleborus* seed is dispersed, the better it germinates. Seed falling directly from the mother plant have the best germination results, with the disadvantage that all the seedlings stand packed next to each other. They can be transplanted after emergence of the first true leaves.

In this way, a larger expanse can be populated with Lenten roses without your having to invest much work or money – though dry periods present a risk, potentially leading to die-off. The important thing is to have a good foundation of plants and nature will take care of the rest. Combine with *Brunnera*, *Symphytum*, *Aquilegia*, *Corydalis* and other long-lived, shade-tolerant perennials to create beautiful garden displays.

Lenten roses are heavy feeders and appreciate regular applications of well-rotted compost that is free of weed seeds. They grow in neutral, humus-rich, loamy soil and appreciate occasional applications of lime. Prerequisites for thriving plants include deep soil, partial shade and location under deep-rooting trees. Fully grown Lenten roses will delight you year after year.

The dame's violet finds good use along woodland edges and between shrubs, growing about 1 m (3¼ ft) tall. While it is described as being short-lived, its life can be extended by lightly pruning the base rosette, encouraging strong, healthy stems. The flowers give off an incomparable aroma of violets during their blooming period of late spring to early summer, especially when they form large groups. Colours range from reddish violet to pure violet or white. *Hesperis* has many closely related species that maintain themselves by self-seeding in light, limy soils; they are easy to control. Good companions include yellow-flowering *Alchemilla mollis* (lady's mantle) and *Patrinia* (late-flowering honeysuckle).

Lunaria
biennial / seed

Meconopsis cambrica
short-lived perennial / plug plant

In the wild, the 50–100 cm (20–40 in) tall white-flowered honesty *Lunaria annua* is a classic woodland valley plant. It therefore prefers shady sites with loose, limy, humus-rich soil that is always somewhat moist.

In spite of what the botanical name implies, *L. annua* is not an annual; it overwinters once and is thus biennial. It is at its most effective in groups. There are white-flowered and violet-flowered varieties, but it is not so much the flowers, which appear from late spring to late summer, that are interesting as the thin, translucent seedpods, which are moon-shaped and the source of the plant's Latin generic name. Honesty is most easily introduced into the garden via seed.

Perennial honesty (*L. rediviva*) can be planted in poor soils in the shade.

Its large, pointed oval leaves are lightly serrated, giving the plant an interesting appearance even when it is not flowering. In contrast to *L. annua*, perennial honesty's seedpods are oblong and not so noticeable. Its bright pink-violet flowers smell wonderful, however. This species is best in larger beds with partial shade where prolific seeding is not a problem.

When the Welsh poppy is in the right spot, it can have a disproportionately large visual effect in the garden. It is found in Wales, Ireland, Spain and parts of France and can sometimes turn into a weed. To stay on top of it, timely pruning of the seed capsules is crucial.

The flowers of *Meconopsis cambrica* have four petals and the basic colour is yellow, though there are also white, orange and double-flowered varieties. They appear in mid to late summer and are 5 cm (2 in) in diameter, borne on stems about 40 cm (16 in) tall.

The seed can be directly sown; patches that are too dense need to be thinned by hand. You can keep the colour uniform by removing individuals of other colours, though groups of mixed colours in partial shade can be attractive.

Milium effusum 'Aureum'
short-lived perennial / seed, plug plant

Bowles's golden grass does not have a spectacular growth habit nor are its 70 cm (28 in) high stems particularly impressive; its ornamental aspect is the luminosity of its yellow foliage in spring, which is striking even when seen from a distance. To enhance this effect, combine with dark-leaved plants or site it in loose groups at the back of a border. This works well because the surrounding plants will not grow tall until much later in the season. The foliage later turns green. The plant self-seeds moderately and likes moist soil. In spring and autumn small seedlings can easily be transplanted.

Pseudofumaria lutea
short-lived perennial / plug plant

Yellow corydalis, which is also known by the botanical name *Corydalis lutea*, is suited to shady, dry patches beneath conifers. Its small yellow flowers are on display for practically the entire growing season, making this plant especially valuable. Just a few plants are enough to establish it in the garden at the right spot. Ants take care of the rest, carrying the seed away for the lipid-rich fleshy structures that stick to its seeds. Yellow corydalis can also be established in rain shadows underneath house eaves and in the joints of stone walls, making pretty flowering mounds that are 20–40 cm (8–16 in) high.

A closely related species is *P. alba*, which has white flowers and similar growth. It can be used in the same way as *P. lutea*. Growing it in pots is not recommended as it does not flourish in this environment.

Pulmonaria mollis
long-lived perennial / plug plant

Lungwort has a good reputation for hardiness and persistence in the garden. This species is by far the largest of the genus and one of the earliest to flower. Its long, silky-haired, tongue-shaped leaves form rosettes of 60 cm (2 ft) diameter and in contrast to other lungworts are not spotted. They are very attractive in summer and are not prone to mildew. The flowers, which are borne in dense heads, range in colour from dark brick red to a greyish purple and at 30 cm (12 in) high they tower over the leaves. The flowering period is from late spring to early summer.

Once established, this lungwort tolerates quite a bit of dryness which is a huge advantage if you want to site it under shrubs and trees. It can be transplanted during dormancy before flowering or later with ripe leaves. It readily self-seeds.

Smyrnium perfoliatum (perfoliate alexander) blooms over a long period of time, though it takes a few years to establish. The attempt is most likely to be successful when using fresh seed. At Great Dixter in England, it thrives with other plants such as *Eryngium* (sea holly), *Bupleurum longifolium* (hare's ear) and *Dipsacus fullonum* (common teasel).

Smyrnium perfoliatum
biennial or short-lived perennial / seed (cold germinating), plug plant

During its flowering period from early to midsummer, the perfoliate alexander is a feast for the eyes because of its unusual appearance. This plant forms leaf rosettes the first year, then the following year produces upright stems more than 1 m (3¼ ft) tall that bear tiny greenish-yellow flowers that are rich in nectar. The leaves, which surround the stems, are mostly the same colour.

The perfoliate alexander is mostly found in the Alps and mountain forests of southern Europe. This umbellifer grows in meagre, dry, well-draining soils in full sun or partial shade; self-seeding only occurs under these conditions.

Tanacetum parthenium
short-lived perennial / seed, plug plant

Feverfew is a perennial with a long history of cultivation, not least for its medicinal benefits. It belongs in every cottage garden and maintains itself through self-seeding for many years. There are single-flowered and double-flowered varieties as well as some with yellow leaves, all self-seeding reliably. Feverfew loves partially shaded, moist locations and, depending on the variety, grows to 50–90 cm (20–36 in) tall, flowering the entire summer. It is ideal for filling gaps in flowerbeds where varieties with yellow foliage will provide extra colour in spring.

Telekia speciosa
long-lived perennial / plug plant

The heart-leaved oxeye comes from southern Europe, northern Turkey and the Caucasus, where it is often found in the shady, damp parts of historical gardens, having maintained itself there for centuries. A row of plants in front of a dark wall of trees or a body of water can look very impressive. In small gardens, a few single plants in the background as foliage interest can work wonders.

The entire plant resembles *Inula magnifica* (giant inula), though its large, light yellow, composite flowers are more radiant, and the heart-shaped, decorative leaves more serrated. At ideal sites, it can grow to nearly 2 m (6½ ft) in height, bearing flowers between early summer and early autumn.

Good, moist, deep soil is required for the plants to thrive. The sunnier the location, the wetter the soil needs to be. This species seeds reliably, but does not become a nuisance.

Tulipa sprengeri

long-lived perennial / plug plant

Sprenger tulip is an unusual member of the *Tulipa* genus, with a late blooming period from late spring to early summer and grass-green leaves. It comes from northern Turkey (where it no longer exists) and prefers open, moist forest edges that are partially shaded during the blooming period. Its propagation strategy explains its high price and tendency to overgrow: unlike most other tulips, it doesn't develop offsets from bulbs and instead produces a large number of viable seeds. It is thus mostly propagated by hobby gardeners and not by the Dutch flower bulb industry. While most wild tulips take six to nine years to produce the first flower, the Sprenger tulip blooms within four years, producing red flowers on stems 30 cm (12 in) tall.

Additional species

Anemone ranunculoides (wood ginger)
Begonia grandis subsp. *evansiana* (beefsteak plant)
Bupleurum rotundifolium (round-leaf hare's ear)
Chionodoxa forbesii (glory-of-the-snow)
Doronicum orientale (leopard's bane)
Scilla siberica (Siberian squill)

The pleasantly sweet-smelling *Eranthis hyemalis*
(winter aconite) is originally from southern
Europe and Asia Minor and has long been planted
in gardens, parks and forest paths. When the soil
is moist in spring and there is no competition – as
underneath summer trees and shrubs – winter
aconite can easily produce plenty of seed. In
some forests, such as Rautal bei Jena, Germany, it
completely carpets the ground.

RESOURCES

Nurseries

United Kingdom

The Beth Chatto Gardens
bethchatto.co.uk

Cotswold Garden Flowers
cgf.net

Dove Cottage Nursery
dovecottagenursery.co.uk

Great Dixter Nurseries
greatdixter.co.uk

Knoll Gardens
knollgardens.co.uk
Nicky's Nursery
nickys-nursery.co.uk

Wildside Nursery
wileyatwildside.com

United States of America

Annie's Annuals
anniesannuals.com

Digging Dog Nursery
diggingdog.com

Greenlee Nursery
greenleenursery.com

Prairie Nursery
prairienursery.com

Canada

Bluestem Nursery
bluestem.ca

Wildflower Farm
wildflowerfarm.com

Gardens to visit

United Kingdom

Derek Jarman's Garden
Prospect Cottage
Dungeness Road, Romney Marsh,
Kent TN29 9NE

Great Dixter
Northiam, Rye, East Sussex TN31 6PH
greatdixter.co.uk

Waltham Place
Church Hill, White Waltham, Berkshire SL6 3JH
walthamplace.com

United States

The Highline
New York City, NY
thehighline.org

The Lurie Garden
Chicago, IL
luriegarden.org

Lady Bird Johnson Wildflower Center
Austin, TX
wildflower.org

Further reading

Austria

Christian Kress (Garden and nursery)
4974 Ort im Innkreis 131, Austria
sarastro-stauden.com

France

Jardin Plume (Garden and nursery)
790 Rue de la Plaine, 76116 Auzouville-sur-Ry,
France
lejardinplume.com

Germany

Fine Molz und Till Hofmann
Beerfeldener Str. 28, 69483 Affolterbach, Germany
die-staudengaertnerei.de

Peter Janke's garden
Hortvs
Hochdahler Strasse 350, 40724 Hilden, Germany
peter-janke-gartenkonzepte.de

Netherlands

Anja and Piet Oudolf's garden
Broekstraat 17, 6999 DE Hummelo, Netherlands
oudolf.com

Madelien van Hasselt's garden
Het Vlackeland
Vlackeweg 5A, 4339 PE, Nieuw en St Joosland,
Zeeland, Niederlande
vlackeland.nl

Ton ter Linden and Gert Tabak's garden
Krûswei 14, 9215 MA De Veenhoop, Netherlands
ateliertonterlinden.nl

Chatto, Beth: *Beth Chatto's Gravel Garden*. Frances
Lincoln, 2000.

Gray, Barbara and Silk, Heather: *Wild Flowers of
Dungeness – A Photographic Guide*. 2007.

Hansen, Richard und Stahl, Friedrich: *Perennials
and their garden habitats*. Cambridge University
Press, 1993.

Jarman, Derek and Sooley, Howard: *Derek Jarman's
Garden*. Thames and Hudson, 1995.

Oudolf, Piet und Kingsbury, Noel: *Planting: A New
Perspective*. Timber Press 2013.

Oudolf, Piet und Kingsbury, Noel: *Planting Design.
Gardens in time and space*. Timber Press, 2005.

Ronan, Frank: *Self-sowing Plants*. The Dixter
Handbooks. Available at greatdixtershop.co.uk

Index

Page numbers in bold indicate the main
description of plant.

A

Achillea millefolium   **152**

Acidification   59

Aconite, winter   **165**, 175

Agrostemma githago   151

Alcea ficifolia   **128**

Alcea rosea   76, **128**, 133

Alchemilla epipsila   122

Alchemilla mollis   90, 121, **129**

Allium   89

Allium aflatunense   67, **141**

Allium carinatum subsp. *pulchellum*   109, 139

Allium schoenoprasum   **140**

Allium sphaerocephalon   109, **153**

Alpine willowherb   21, **132**

Althaea cannabina   **153**

Ammi majus   151

Anemone blanda   58

Anemone nemorosa   **162**, 168

Anemone, wood   **162**, 168

Anethum graveolens   63, 151

Angelica archangelica   25, 118, 151

Angelica gigas   151

Angelica, garden   25, 118, 151

Angelica, purple   151

Annual plants   23

Anthemis tinctoria   130, **153**, 154

Anthericum ramosum   **154**

Anthriscus sylvestris 'Raven's Wing'   **154**

Antirrhinum   **129**, 138

Antirrhinum braun-blanquetii   **129**

Antirrhinum majus   36, **129**

Aquilegia   89, **169**

Aquilegia caerulea   11

Aquilegia vulgaris   122, **141**

Arion vulgaris   102

Artemisia   **156**

Artemisia absinthium   **154**

Artemisia ludoviciana var. *latiloba*   125

Atriplex hortensis var. *rubra*   63, 67, 72, **142**

Avoidance   20

B

Balsam, Himalayan   82

Barley, annual foxtail   64, 67, 72, 132, **135**

Bee balm   145

Bellflower   **163**

Bellflower, pendulous   161

Bentonite   94

Bergamot, wild   **145**

Biennial plants   25

Black box   11

Blanket flower   **134**

Bluebell, Spanish   167

Bog garden   59

Bowles's golden grass   **171**

Briza maxima   114, 136, 139

Brown-eyed susan   53

Brunnera   **169**

Brunnera macrophylla   **163**, 167

Bucket   90

Bulbs   47

Bullwort   151

Bupleurum aureum   155, **156**

Bupleurum rotundifolium   **174**

Burnet   **160**

C

Calamagrostis brachytricha   153, **156**

Calcium carbonate   57

Calendula officinalis   76, 151

Campanula   **163**

Campanula persicifolia   103, 109, **142**

Campanula rapunculoides   **163**

Campanula trachelium   **163**

Caper bush   **166**

Castilleja linariifolia   11

Centaurea cyanus   22

Centaurea montana   **151**

Centranthus ruber   36, 39, 40, 64, 72, 76, 81, 92, 103, 111, 114, **130**

Chamomile, dyer's   130, **153**

Chicory   7

Chinese silver grass   26

Chives **140**

Cichorium intybus 7

Clary, Balkan 75, 103, **149**

Clary sage 72, 109, **138**

Clary, whorled **160**

Columbine 86, **169**

Competition 16

Coneflower, 'Goldsturm' **159**

Coneflower, Deam's **159**

Conium maculatum 122

Coreopsis tinctoria 151

Corn cockle 151

Cornflower 22

Cortia wallichiana **163**

Corydalis **169**

Corydalis solida subsp. *transsylvanica* **164**, 168

Corydalis, yellow 16, **171**

Cotton lavender 40

Cotton thistle 103, **146**

Cowslip 161

Crambe maritima 29, 32, 40, **130**

Cranesbill, dusky **168**

Cranesbill, meadow **156**

Crocosmia 68, 71, 121

Crocus **164**

Crocus tommasinianus **164**

Crushed limestone bed 94

Cyclamen **165**

D

Daisy, ox-eye 83, 90, **157**, 158

Dame's violet **169**

Deschampsia cespitosa 26, 67, 68, 71, **165**

Deserts 19

Dianthus cruentus **154**

Digitalis grandiflora **142**

Digitalis purpurea 20, 25, 35, 40, **142**, 147

Dill 63, 151

Dipsacus fullonum 68, 83, **144**

Disturbance 16

Disturbance sites 19

Dolomitic lime 57

Dungeness 29, 31

Dutch Wave 86, 111

Dyer's rocket 35

E

Echinops sphaerocephalus 161

Echium **154**

Echium russicum **130**

Echium vulgare 36, **130**

Ecokathedraal 55

Eggshells 57

Epilobium dodonaei 21, **132**

Eranthis 162, 164

Eranthis hyemalis **165**, 175

Erigeron karvinskianus 81, 92, **131**

Eryngium 130, 144

Eryngium giganteum 103, **131**

Eschscholzia **132**, 146

Eschscholzia californica 39, 130, 132, 136

Eschscholzia mexicana 17

Euphorbia dulcis 'Chameleon' **166**

Euphorbia epithymoides **144**

Euphorbia griffithii 121

Euphorbia lathyris **166**

Euphorbia myrsinites **132**

Euphorbia polychroma **144**

Evening primrose 84, **137**

Evening primrose, Mexican 151

Evening primrose, red-sepal 53, 72, 151

F

Feather grass 130, 132, 154, 156

Feather grass, Mexican 64, 67, 111, 114, 117, **137**

Feather reed grass, Korean 153, **156**

Fennel 70, 105, 107, 125

Fennel, bronze **144**

Feverfew **173**

Flax, perennial 154, **157**

Flower pot 51

Flowering allium 89

Flowering onion 67, **141**

Foeniculum vulgare 70, 105, 107, 125

Foeniculum vulgare 'Purpureum' **144**

Foxglove, purple 20, 25, 35, 40, **142**, 147

Foxglove, yellow **142**

Fritillaria meleagris   100
Fumewort   **164**, 168

G

Gaillardia aristata   **134**
Galanthus   56, 162
Galanthus nivalis   **166**
Garlic, keeled   103, 109
Garlic, round-headed   109, **153**
Gaura   **156**
Gaura lindheimeri   130, **134**, 146, 153
Gaura, white   130, **134**, 146, 153
Geophytes   47
Geranium clarkei   **157**
Geranium himalayense   **157**
Geranium phaeum   **168**
Geranium pratense   **156**
Geranium robertianum   55
Geranium sanguineum   **154**
Gerritsen, Henk   86, 111
Giant hog fennel   111, 114, 117, **137**
Giant sea holly   103, **131**
Glaucium flavum   35, 40, 139
Golden tickseed   151
Gorse   36
Gravel gardens   56
Great blue-bottle   151
Great Dixter   14, 81, 83, 90, 92, 97
Grime, John Philip   16

H

Hapaxanths   25
Hare's ear   155, **156**
Hasselt, Madelien van   63
Hawkweed, spotted   103, 111, 135
Hawkweed, shaggy   47, **135**
Heart-leaved oxeye   68, 103, 106, **173**
Helianthemum   **130**
Helianthus   26
Heliopsis helianthoides var. *scabra*   161
Hellebore, holly-leaved   75, 103, **134**
Hellebore, stinking   134, **168**
Helleborus   **164**
Helleborus argutifolius   75, 103, **134**
Helleborus foetidus   134, **168**
Helleborus × *hybridus*   **169**
Helleborus orientalis   27
Hemlock, poison   122
Hemlock, striped   151
Herb robert   55
Hesperis matronalis   **169**
Hibiscus cannabinus   151
Hieracium maculatum   103, 111, **135**
Hieracium villosum   47, **135**
Hofmann, Till   108
Hollyhock   76, **128**, 133
Honesty, annual   **170**
Honeyplant, golden   **161**
Hordeum jubatum   64, 67, 72, 132, **135**

Horehound   75
Hornpoppy, yellow   35, 40, 139
Hyacinth, broad-leaved grape   139
Hyacinthoides hispanica   167
Hypericum olympicum   114

I

Impatiens glandulifera   82
Inula magnifica   84, 125, **173**
Inula, giant   84, 125, **173**
Invasive plants   81
Iris spuria   35
Iris, wild   35
Isatis tinctoria   139

J

Jacob's ladder   **159**
Jardin Plume   84
Jarman, Derek   39

K

Kenaf   151
Knautia macedonica   67, 75, 76, 109, 130, **145**
Kniphofia   36, 40, 64
Krehl, Beatrice   111
Kühn, Norbert   21
Kunick, Wolfram   53

L

Lady's mantle 90, **129**

Lathyrus latifolius 36

Lenten rose, hybrid **169**

Leopard plant 71

Leucanthemum vulgare 83, 90, **157**, 158

Life spans 23

Ligularia dentata 71

Lime 57

Limestone, crushed 94

Linaria purpurea 36, 72, **135**

Linden, Ton ter 88, 89

Linum austriacum 154, **157**

Linum perenne 154, **157**

Long-lived perennials 27

Love-in-a-mist 68, 104, **146**, 147

Lunaria **170**

Lunaria annua **170**

Lunaria rediviva **170**

Lungwort **171**

Lupin 11, 118, 151

Lupin, Coulter's 17

Lupinus 118, 151

Lupinus argenteus 11

Lupinus sparsiflorus 17

Lythrum salicaria 72

M

Marigold 76, 151

Marrubium incanum 75

Meadows 96

Meconopsis cambrica **170**

Melica transsilvanica 109

Mexican feather grass 64, 67, 111, 114, 117, **137**

Mexican fleabane 81, 92, **131**

Milium effusum 'Aureum' **171**

Miscanthus sinensis 26

Miss Willmott's ghost 103, **131**

Molinia arundinacea 161

Molopospermum peloponnesiacum 151

Molz, Fine 108

Monarda fistulosa subsp. *menthifolia* 145

Monocarpic plants 25

Montbretia 68, 71, 121

Moon carrot **138**

Moor-grass, purple 161

Moss 56, 58

Mount Olympus St John's wort 114

Mulch, mineral 108

Mullein 6, 53, 63, 68, 70, 98, 109, 111, 136, 151, 154, 161

Muscari latifolium 139

Mussels 54, 57, 75, 76

Mycorrhiza 59

Myosotis sylvatica **146**

N

Nassella tenuissima 64, 67, 111, 114, 117, **137**

Needle litter 59

Niche plants 16

Nigella damascena 68, 104, **146**, 147

North American ox-eye 161

O

Oenothera glazioviana 53, 72, 151

Oenothera odorata 84, **137**

Oenothera versicolor 151

Onopordum acanthium 103, **146**

Oppenheimer, Carlota 113

Oppenheimer, Strilli 111

Orach, red 63, 67, 72, **142**

Oregano 114, 125

Origanum 114

Origanum laevigatum 'Hopley' 125

Orlaya grandiflora **148**

Oudolf, Piet 86

P

Paeonia obovata 101

Palm-leaf marshmallow 153

Papaver atlanticum 161

Papaver rhoeas 19, 36, 67, 72, 121, 151

Papaver somniferum 35, 67, 83, 121, 147, **148**

Parsley, cow **154**

Parsley, milk **163**

Parsnip 72, 118, 121, 151

Pastinaca sativa 72, 118, 121, 151

Patrinia **169**

Patrinia scabiosifolia 161

Pea, broad-leaved everlasting 36

Penstemon 137, 138

Penstemon digitalis 'Husker Red' 161

Peony, obovate 101

Perfoliate alexander 172, **173**

Peucedanum verticillare 111, 114, 117, **137**

Pioneer plants 26

Polemonium caeruleum **159**

Poppy, atlas 161

Poppy, California 39, 130, 132, 136

Poppy, corn 19, 36, 67, 72, 121, 151

Poppy, opium 35, 67, 83, 121, 147, **148**

Poppy, Welsh **170**

Primula veris subsp. *veris* 161

Propagation, generative 81

Propagation, vegetative 81

Pseudofumaria alba **171**

Pseudofumaria lutea 16, **171**

Pulmonaria mollis **171**

Purple loosestrife 72

Purple toadflax 36, 72, **135**

Q

Quaking grass, greater 114, 136, 139

Quicklime 57

R

Ranunculus ficaria **168**

Rattle 96, 97

Red-hot pokers 36, 40, 64

Reseda alba 75

Reseda luteola 35

Rhinanthus 96, 97

Rock flour 57

Rose campion 72, 118, 122, **150**

Roy, Louis le 55

Rubble, construction 57

Rudbeckia fulgida var. *deamii* **159**

Rudbeckia fulgida var. *sullivantii* **159**

Rudbeckia hirta 53

Rudbeckia laciniata **159**

Rudbeckia subtomentosa **159**

Rudbeckia triloba **149**

Ruderal flora 26

Rumex acetosa 121

S

Sage, clary 103, **149**

Sage, wood 75

Salsify, purple 22, 121, **150**

Salt 59

Salvia aethiopis **149**

Salvia amplexicaulis **149**

Salvia argentea **149**

Salvia hakusanensis **160**

Salvia nemorosa 103, **149**

Salvia nutans **149**

Salvia obtusa **160**

Salvia sclarea 72, 109, **138**

Salvia × sylvestris 'Blauhügel' 75

Salvia verticillata **160**

Sanguisorba **160**

Sanguisorba officinalis **160**

Sanguisorba tenuifolia var. *alba* **160**

Santolina chamaecyparissus 40

Scabiosa ochroleuca 151

Scabious, Macedonian 67, 75, 76, 109, 130, **145**

Scabious, pale yellow 151

Scandix pecten-veneris 151

Sea kale 29, 32, 40, **130**

Sedum 75, **130**

Sedum acre 36

Seed 47

Seed bed 49

Seed tray 50

Selinum wallichianum **163**

Semelparous organisms 25

Seseli gummiferum **138**

Shepherd's needle 151
Short-lived perennials 26
Silene coronaria 72, 118, 122, **150**
Silene viscaria **150**
Silver Summer 108
Slugs 102
Smyrnium perfoliatum 172, **173**
Snake's head fritillary 100
Snapdragon 36, **129**, 138
Snowdrop 56, 162, **166**
Soil 48
Soil pH, adjusting 57, 59
Sorrel, common 121
Spider plant **154**
Spire, red 109
Sprenger tulip **174**
Spurge 121
Spurge, broad-leaved glaucous **132**
Spurge, many-coloured **144**
Spurge, sweet **166**
Sticky catchfly **150**
Stipa 130, 132, 154, 156
Stipa calamagrostis 153
Stonecrop 130
Stonecrop, biting 36
Stonecrop, white 36
Strategies 20
Stress 20
Succession 26

Sunflower, perennial 26
Surface structure 56
Symphyandra pendula 161
Symphytum **169**

T
Tanacetum parthenium **173**
Teasel, common 68, 83, **144**
Telekia speciosa 68, 103, 106, **173**
Thistle, globe 161
Tragopogon porrifolius 22, 121, **150**
Tufted hairgrass 26, 67, 68, 71, **165**

U
Ulex europaeus 36
Underground profiling 60
Underground storage organs 47

V
Valerian, eastern 161
Valerian, garden 161
Valerian, red 36, 39, 40, 64, 72, 76, 81, 92, 103, 111, 114, **130**
Valeriana officinalis 161
Verbascum 7, 53, 63, **151**, 154
Verbascum bombyciferum 109, 111, 136, 151
Verbascum chaixii 98
Verbascum densiflorum **151**
Verbascum nigrum 68, 70

Verbascum olympicum **151**
Verbascum phoeniceum **151**, 161
Verbena bonariensis 64, 72, 104, **139**, 151
Verbena hastata 63, 70, 103, **151**
Verbesina alternifolia **161**
Vervain, Argentinian 64, 72, 104, **139**, 151
Viola odorata 13
Violet 13
Viper's bugloss 36, **130**

W
Waltham Place 111
Weld 35
White laceflower **148**
White mignonette 75
White peat 56, 59
Winter windflower 58
Woad 139
Wood forget-me-not **146**
Wormwood **154**

Y
Yarrow **152**

Z
Zetterlund, Henrik 101
Zinnia peruviana 151
Zinnia, Peruvian 151

Afterword and acknowledgements

A book should never be prescriptive but instead provide an inspiring starting point from which new ideas develop. This is especially true of *Cultivating Chaos*. The plants and locations described here are based on our experiences but there are no absolutes. We have often noticed that some species grow brilliantly in one garden while in another, sometimes located just a few metres away, they sulk for no apparent reason.

We hope that *Cultivating Chaos* will awaken in you the desire to observe and experiment with plants. If a particular species doesn't thrive, try it again next year – perhaps under somewhat different conditions. And if it doesn't work the second time, try it a third. If you still can't get it to grow, then simply rejoice in the plants that do like to grow in your garden.

We are interested in your experiences. Please send them to gartenpraxis@ulmer.de (subject: BBG Hinweise) or Verlag Eugen Ulmer, Redaktion "Gartenpraxis", Keyword: Blackbox Gardening, Wollgrasweg 41, 70599 Stuttgart, Germany.

The existence of this book is first and foremost due to the understanding of spouses, partners and children, who allowed us enough time, gave us support and, when necessary, insisted we take creative breaks.

For technical and factual support, we would like to thank Heike and Dieter Gaissmayer, Fergus Garrett, Madelien van Hasselt, Beatrice Krehl, Norbert Kühn, Wolfram Kunick, Ton ter Linden and Gert Tabak, Fine Molz and Till Hofmann, Strilli and Nicky Oppenheimer, and Jörg Pfenningschmidt. If we have forgotten anybody, please forgive us and get in touch.

The authors

Jonas Reif is editor-in-chief of the German gardening magazine *Gartenpraxis* and lives in Zeuthen near Berlin. An adventurous landscape architect and passionate hobby gardener, Reif is constantly creating new approaches to lively, diverse plantings in municipal parks as well as in his own garden.

Christian Kress is the proprietor of the plant nursery Sarastro-Stauden, located in Ort im Innkreis, Austria, one of today's most important nurseries for gardening aficionados in central Europe. Kress trained as an ornamental gardener, studied to be a horticultural technician and has completed internships in several different countries. In addition to his plant-breeding work, where he has developed many of his own varieties, Kress is well known for the numerous articles he has authored and his highly respected newsletter.

Jürgen Becker lives in Hilden, Germany and is one of the most successful garden photographers in the world. His photographs have been published in a multitude of calendars, books and renowned magazines. Becker began his career as a freelance photographer after studying at the Kunstakademie in Düsseldorf. He has received several international awards for his work, including "Photographer of the Year" (2010 and 2012) from the Garden Media Guild in London.

Photo credits

Published in 2015 by Timber Press, Inc.

The Haseltine Building
133 S.W. Second Avenue, Suite 450
Portland, Oregon 97204-3527
timberpress.com

For details on other Timber Press books and to sign up for
our newsletters, please visit our website, timberpress.com.

Cover photo by Jürgen Becker
Printed in Germany

ISBN 978-1-60469-652-3

Catalogue records for this book are available from the
British Library and the Library of Congress.